R00164 83127

CHICAGO PUBLIC LIBRARY
HAROLD WASHINGTON LIBRARY CENTER

R0016483127

D1544231

Benefits and Burdens

LEBANON

Golan Heights

SY[R]

Lake Tiberias

TERRITORY OCCUPIED BY ISRAEL
SINCE JUNE 1967

Galilee

⚑ Haifa

ISRAEL

MEDITERRANEAN SEA

Jordan River

● Jenin

Samaria

● Tulkarm

Nablus ●

Damiya Bridge

EAST BANK

Tel Aviv
Jaffa

WEST BANK

A[m]

● Ramallah

Allenby Bridge

Jerusalem

JORD[AN]

● Bethlehem

Dead Sea

● Hebron

Judea

● Gaza

Gaza Strip

[A]rish

Negev

[E]GYPT

0   MILES

Benefits and Burdens:
A Report on the West Bank and Gaza Strip Economies Since 1967

Brian Van Arkadie

With a prologue by Larry L. Fabian

CARNEGIE ENDOWMENT FOR INTERNATIONAL PEACE
NEW YORK   WASHINGTON, D.C.

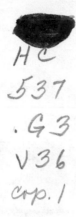

HC
537
.G3
V36
crp. 1

© 1977, Carnegie Endowment for International Peace. All rights reserved, including the right to reproduce this book or portions thereof in any form, except
for the inclusion of brief quotations in a review. All inquiries should be addressed
to the Carnegie Endowment for International Peace, 11 Dupont Circle, N.W.,
Washington, D.C. 20036 or 345 East 46th Street, New York, New York 10017.

I.S.B.N.   0-87003-006-X

Library of Congress Catalog Card Number: 76-57443

Printed in the United States of America.

BUSINESS/SCIENCE/TECHNOLOGY DIVISION
THE CHICAGO PUBLIC LIBRARY
MAY 2 6 1978

Contents

Preface

In 1975 as part of its new Middle East Program under the direction of Larry L. Fabian, the Carnegie Endowment decided to undertake an appraisal of the economic consequences of the Israeli occupation of the West Bank and Gaza Strip. Since 1967 the economic life of the Palestinian population in these territories has undergone substantial transformation, as have their economic connections with both Israel and Jordan. The economic meaning of this transformation is neither obvious nor uniformly interpreted by those affected. The political implications are even more controversial.

In the context of possible progress towards a negotiated Middle East settlement the international discussion continues to intensify about the status of the West Bank and the Gaza Strip. To provide background for that discussion, we asked Brian Van Arkadie to join the Endowment to assess the principal economic trends affecting the two territories. In doing so he has identified the fundamental economic conditions and interests that have emerged in recent years. Moreover, he has framed his appraisal in terms that could be meaningful as a baseline for thinking about the future of the West Bank and the Gaza Strip.

Van Arkadie, who was associated with the Endowment while conducting this study, is now professor of economic development and deputy rector of the Institute of Social Studies in the Hague, Netherlands. When he began his Carnegie assignment he was a fellow of Queens' College at Cambridge University and director of that university's Centre for Latin American Studies. During a varied professional career, he has worked for an extended period as an economic advisor in East Africa, was for a short time a British civil servant, and has acted as an economic consultant to a number of international agencies. He has also taught economics at Yale University and Dartmouth College and in Britain at the Institute of Development Studies, University of Sussex. He graduated from the London School of Economics and was awarded his Ph.D. from the University of California at Berkeley.

As always, Endowment sponsorship of this study implies a belief only in the importance of the subject. The views expressed are those of the author. Comments or inquiries on this and other work of the Endowment may be addressed to the office of the Carnegie Endowment for International Peace, 345 East 46th Street, New York, New York 10017, or 11 Dupont Circle, N.W., Washington, D.C. 20036.

Thomas L. Hughes
President
Carnegie Endowment for International Peace

Author's Preface

When I agreed in the spring of 1975 to produce this report at the request of the Carnegie Endowment, I was aware that my own background and the subject-matter under study both would define how the study would be carried out.

My background is that of an economist who has specialized in development problems, having worked as an academic and government economist in various parts of the world—but not in the Middle East. I approached this new assignment with a background of experience in interpreting statistical data and in dealing with the range of available views concerning relations between rich and poor regions. While I was able, during 1975, to gain vivid first-hand impressions of Israel, the West Bank, the Gaza Strip, and Jordan, my visits were relatively brief. Moreover, my schedule for completing this study was tight. Because of this limited time and the complexity of the economic situation I was able to observe, I was wary of drawing too many conclusions from my direct impressions.

In practice, therefore, I have relied heavily on the interpretation of documentary and, more particularly, statistical sources—the quality and inadequacies of which I discuss in the text of the study. I also have relied largely on sources that are published or, in a few instances, fairly readily accessible, at least in the Middle

East. These have mostly been English-language materials, although selected Hebrew and Arabic sources were translated specifically for this research.

For judging the overall economic situation, the use of macro-statistical data is undoubtedly more satisfactory than isolated impressions of particular, but limited, successes or failures. However, for certain economic features of the situation under study, statistical data are sparse or macro-economic observation too general to expose relevant details. For example, the internal commercial and financial workings of the West Bank and the Gaza Strip economies cannot be satisfactorily understood from available statistical or other published sources. In instances of this kind, the absence of longstanding and intimate personal acquaintance is a liability, but the instances are not, in my judgment, numerous enough to be a serious constraint on the overall analysis. For the most part, the crucial economic changes that have occurred since 1967, in the West Bank and the Gaza Strip as well as in their connections with the Israeli and Jordanian economies, all have been large enough so that the main trends can be clearly delineated, even allowing for a generous degree of unreliability in the available data.

In view of my heavy reliance on statistical sources it is important for me to point out two methodological considerations that have affected the scope of this study.

First, there is some unavoidable time lag in the data on which the analysis is based. When the first draft of the manuscript was completed, the data available to me gave an overview of the economic situation only up to the end of 1973. Some information on 1974—*e.g.,* concerning the employment situation—was also in hand at this time. I have attempted to include in the tables the important part of this data so that the reader will be able to judge the sources available to me at the time of writing.

At the final stages of work on the manuscript, data published in Israel in 1976 became available to me. It was not possible to update all tables and calculations without incurring undue delay; however, at appropriate places in the study I refer to one important, more recent factor—the expansion of private investment in the West Bank during 1974. Not to have brought this particular phenomenon into the picture would have created a significantly false impression. Other than this, in my view, the more recently available data have not changed the basic judgments offered in the study.

Second, there is a major omission in the structure of the

study. I do not discuss either the economic aspects of the Israeli population settlements in the occupied territories or the economic implications of Israeli land acquisition there. The significance of both is great, the controversy over both is intense, and as every student of the Middle East knows, the history of the region for many decades has been intimately linked to questions of land and population—during the Palestine Mandate period, from 1948 to 1967, and since the Six Day War. But any analyst with limited time and resources faces the very practical reality that there simply is no readily accessible data to support careful assessment of the strictly economic dimension of either of these subjects. Both subjects are too important to be treated offhandedly or impressionistically. On balance, therefore, the omission of both seemed the more prudent decision—although a difficult one. As far as the Israeli settlements are concerned, this decision can be justified at least partly because available evidence suggests that, their political importance notwithstanding, the post-1967 settlements are still a relatively minor part of the pattern of purely *economic* connections and interactions that have evolved between Israel and the occupied territories to date. As for Israeli land acquisition—especially in and around the formerly Jordanian sector of Jerusalem and at other West Bank locations—reliable economic information in the public domain is even more sketchy than information concerning the settlements. The same methodological constraints operate therefore, even though the little available information suggests that a truly comprehensive survey of the economic aspects of Israel's policies toward the occupied territories would definitely have to take account of the extent and consequences of land acquisition since 1967.

These omissions excepted, the data are sufficiently available and reliable to permit me to fulfill the Carnegie Endowment's terms of reference for this study.

I could not have completed this project in the relatively brief time at my disposal without the indispensible assistance of Eric J. Hooglund, who was until recently a member of the Middle East Program staff at the Endowment, and who is now on the faculty of Bowdoin College in Brunswick, Maine. He gathered essential background information before I began my work. He helped fill in numerous data gaps during the course of the research and writing. And he was a constructive critic at every stage of the final drafting.

September, 1976   Brian Van Arkadie

Prologue:
The Political Setting

BY LARRY L. FABIAN

Since the October 1973 war, Middle East diplomacy has fastened public attention on the Golan Heights and the Sinai Peninsula, the battlegrounds for Arab and Israeli armies in October, 1973. As flash points threatening new war, they were the arenas for Henry Kissinger's step-by-step strategy of achieving military disengagement agreements on the two fronts in 1974 and the Sinai II Pact a year later. To the casual reader of headlines, these territorial stakes seemed to symbolize what the Arab-Israeli conflict is all about.

This perception was jolted in late 1975 and early 1976 by reminders that peace prospects in the Middle East are also tied intimately to developments affecting a third front: on the West Bank of the Jordan and in the Gaza Strip. In these areas, including the formerly Jordanian sector of Jerusalem annexed by Israel in 1967, live the largest concentration of Palestinians under the dominion of a single sovereign anywhere in the world—more than one million Palestinians who have been under Israeli military occupation since the two territories were captured from Jordan and Egypt during the 1967 war. The reminders that dramatized the importance of this front are these:

- The United States went on record in November, 1975, with its first comprehensive policy statement on the Palestinian issue since the October war—the highly controversial Saunders Document. The United States said that the issue must be dealt with in the context of a Middle East peace settlement and implied that none of the plausible solutions from Washington's point of view included continued Israeli retention of the West Bank and the Gaza Strip.

- Not many months afterwards, the U.S. ambassador to the United Nations revived language not used for several years by U.S. officials. His message was that the United States continues to believe that the future of Jerusalem is to be determined not by Israel's unilateral annexation but by future negotiations; that the United States does not recognize the legality of Israeli civilian population settlements anywhere in the occupied territories, including ast Jerusalem; that the United States does not regard such settlements as prejudging the outcome of boundary negotiations between Middle East states; and that the United States regards the presence of these settlements as an obstacle to productive peace negotiations.

- Early in 1976 the Palestinians living in East Jerusalem and major towns on the West Bank raised some of the most violent and sustained anti-Israel protests in the nine-year history of the occupation. Against the background of these disturbances, which were triggered by highly explosive local issues and which attracted worldwide publicity, the West Bank Palestinians took the opportunity of Israeli-administered elections in the territory to vote into municipal office an overwhelming number of nationalistic politicians.

- Subsequently the Gush Emunim movement, vanguard of Israel's religious and nationalist Right, by pressing their campaign for the establishment of settlements, underlined more firmly than ever before their opposition to return of the occupied territories to Arab rule, and to any restrictions by the government of Israel on the right of Israelis to set up new settlements there.

- The impact of these developments was heightened by the

worst outbreak of violence in the twenty-eight-year history of the state of Israel between the country's security force and its Arab citizens living in the Galilee—an outbreak also triggered by local issues and fueled partly by the infectious and volatile climate associated with new assertiveness among Palestinians in the occupied territories.

These events not only reflect the political tension in the Israeli-Palestinian relationship today, they also bring into sharp relief underlying features of the Middle East situation, anticipated nearly three-quarters of a century ago by a distinguished writer on Arab nationalism, Neguib Azoury. He penned a famous forecast that Middle East historians often quote:

> Two important phenomena of the same nature, yet antagonistic, manifest themselves nowadays in Turkish Asia, but have attracted very little attention. They are the awakening of the Arab nation and the latent efforts of the Jews to reconstitute, on a large scale, the ancient Kingdom of Israel. These two movements are destined to fight each other continually. [1]

Thirty years after Azoury's forecast the antagonism had deepened, and a British royal commission under the chairmanship of Lord Peel was charged with reaching a verdict on the rival claims of Jews and Arabs in historic Palestine. In a 1937 report still regarded as the most lucid diagnosis of the Palestine problem in that generation, the commission posed the elemental question that even today remains unanswered between Israeli Jews and Palestinian Arabs: Which of them in the end will govern the land? It is a bedrock question, set deep in the history of these two peoples, shaped heavily by the politics of twentieth century Palestine, and layered over by decades of violence, suffering, and mistrust.

Peel and his colleagues undertook their mission at a time when the British-administered League of Nations Mandate for Palestine was collapsing in three-way civil disorder among the Jews and Arabs of Palestine and the British Mandate authority. The Peel Commission answered the basic question crisply: Neither would govern the whole land of Palestine. The commission proposed a solution that boils down to a single word, still one of the most contentious in the Middle East lexicon—partition. This appeared to be the only way out of what the commission described as the "irrepressible conflict" that had ripened "between two national communities within the narrow bounds of one small country." Partition appeared to be the only way to take account of each community's "national aspirations," which then loomed as "the greatest bar to peace," in a conflict "as much about the future as the present."[2]

The geographic area of the British Mandate for Palestine, to which Lord Peel's verdict was to apply, encompassed what is today the state of Israel, the West Bank, and the Gaza Strip. An area east of the Jordan River was, after World War I, originally part of the British Mandate, the precise eastern boundaries being left for subsequent determination. The area east of the river was designated in 1922 as the separate Emirate of Transjordan, was administered separately thereafter from the Palestine Mandate west of the river, and was excluded by Britain from the application of the Balfour Declaration of 1917 promising a Jewish national home in Palestine. These decisions had been incorporated into the final draft of the Palestine Mandate officially accepted by the League of Nations in 1922 and entered into force in 1923.

The Peel Commission predicted correctly that the Jewish and the Arab communities would both reject partition in the immediate future. Although the Zionist leadership agreed to consider the possibility of partition while rejecting the specific Peel scheme, it was not until after World War II that a detailed partition proposal elicited formal approval from that leadership. The plan—rejected then by the Arabs, as the Peel proposals had been in 1937—was embodied in the U.N. Partition Resolution of 1947, which assigned part of Mandate Palestine to a Jewish state, part to a Palestinian Arab state, and part—including the whole of Jerusalem—to an international trusteeship. With the ensuing Middle East war of 1948-49, Mandate Palestine was finally partitioned—by the sword. A newly independent Israel held, at the end of the war, the territory bounded by the 1949 armistice lines—that is, the borders of Israel before June 4, 1967. Egypt took the Gaza Strip and established a special administration over it. Jordan annexed the West Bank, including East Jerusalem, which had been captured by the Arab Legion during the war, an annexation never recognized by most of the international community.

Peel's commission had made another prognosis that was essentially accurate but off in its timing by a generation or so. After 1948, the conflict between the Jews of Israel and the Palestinians did not steadily worsen, as the commission thought it would. The conflict between the protagonists of the mandate period lapsed instead into a kind of political limbo after 1948, superseded by a dominant and relentless confrontation between Israel and neighboring Arab states. The 1948 war left some Palestinian Arabs inside Israel; they became the backbone of Israel's present Arab population of 450,000 who have held Israeli citizenship since the establishment of the state. Other Palestinians remained in their West Bank and Gaza Strip homes or fled as refugees to those territories. Still other refugees dispersed to Lebanon, Jordan, Syria and elsewhere in the Arab world and beyond. In these circumstances, the Palestinians could not carry on their struggle against Israel without the patronage of the Arab states on whom they became increasingly dependent—a dependence already evident in the early 1940s. The earlier issues between the Arabs of Palestine and the Jews now sovereign in Israel were submerged, manipulated, and postponed. What had previously been a civil war between rival communities during the mandate now was transformed into a succession of inter-state wars between Israel and its neighboring Arab states.

It was the 1967 war and its political aftermath that pulled the relatively dormant historical clash out of this political limbo. And it was the 1973 war and its aftermath that brought the conflict judged by the Peel Commission to be "inherent in the situation from the outset" back onto the center stage in the Middle East. No longer is there a simple either/or choice in arguments about whether the Israeli-Palestinian conflict is more or less crucial than the conflict between Israel and the existing Arab states. In practical terms, the two dimensions are now inextricably intertwined. No resolution of the Palestinian question could be sustained except in a Middle East where Israel and the major Arab states are moving toward some accommodation. And if it is wishful thinking to believe that a solution to the Palestinian question will in itself bring peace to the Middle East, it is no less wishful to believe that progress toward peace is possible without a mutually acceptable accommodation between the Israelis and the Palestinians.

What the 1967 war did was to reopen the debate about partition. Ironically, Israel's stunning military victory was the catalyst. By its territorial acquisitions on the Egyptian and Jordanian fronts, Israel took control for the first time of what had been the entirety of the British-administered Palestine Mandate. The war created the first political vacuum since 1948 in the West Bank, East Jerusalem, and the Gaza Strip. Israel sought almost immediately to fill the vacuum in East Jerusalem through annexation. But at the same time Israel's official policy-declarations nourished an expectation that other newly-won territories would be returned to Arab hands in the context of a peace settlement. And Israel's acceptance of the famous U.N. Resolution 242 affirmed the principle of territorial withdrawal in exchange for secure and recognized boundaries. Seen from this perspective, Resolution 242 was a doctrinal foundation for the repartition of the former area of Mandate Palestine through a process of negotiations in the circumstances prevailing after the Six Day War. The fine-tuning of interpretations of the resolution—all territories? some territories? who goes first? under what conditions? step-by-step or comprehensively?—have all amounted to a *de facto* agenda for negotiating repartition. The negotiations have yet to begin. But attitudes about the terms of repartition began, immediately after the 1967 war—in Israel, in the Palestinian community, and in Jordan.

Not all quarters acknowledge that the principle of repartition is still relevant. That the land of the former Palestine Mandate should be governed by a single sovereign is the fundamental position of those Israelis who insist that for historical, religious, or security reasons no conquered territory be returned; and it is the position of those Palestinians who insist that there must be neither strategic nor even tactical compromise with the goal of regaining the whole of Palestine and establishing a democratic secular state on the ruins of a Zionist Israel. For Israelis in this group, the concept of partition has validity only in the context of sanctioning a repartition of the original area of the mandate in Palestine before 1922, before the region east of the Jordan River was separated from the mandate; thus most of them would acknowledge repartition at the river, but nowhere west of it.

Not all who agree that repartition is acceptable in principle agree in practice on where new lines should be drawn. Many Israelis in the country's ruling establishment, for example, regard favorably the concept articulated by Foreign Minister Yigal Allon, who calls for Israeli retention of about one-third of the West Bank for security reasons—mostly along the Jordan Valley and at strategic points in the relatively unpopulated areas. The so-called Allon plan would return the rest of the West Bank, as a demilitarized Arab enclave, to Jordanian sovereignty in the context of a peace agreement. Meanwhile Israeli paramilitary settlements would be set up in the areas regarded as strategically important under the plan, a precept that has in fact guided the establishment of over twenty government-approved settlements in the West

Bank, most of them in the Jordan Valley Rift, several in the populated highlands. Although some Jordanian and West Bank Palestinian leaders would accept minor changes in the 1967 borders in Israel's favor, few would accept any partition of the West Bank as ambitious as Allon's, and fewer still would regard the maintenance of the *status quo* in Jerusalem as legitimate.

Nor do all who agree that repartition is acceptable in principle agree in practice on whether the result should be two or three states in the area. Israel's "oral doctrine" for the territories held since 1967 has been affirmed regularly: Jerusalem must remain united and the capital of Israel; the Gaza Strip must not revert to Arab control even in a full peace settlement; there must be one and only one Arab state bordering Israel on the east, its boundaries based on agreement between Israel and Jordan, and its political framework such that Palestinian political self-expression can be satisfied within this Jordanian arrangement. At times during the intricate ebb and flow of West Bank politics since 1967, Palestinians there have expressed support for an independent state separate from Israel and Jordan—an alternative that reflected both an obvious wish to end the Israeli occupation and a reaction to the souring of Jordanian-Palestinian relations after Jordan's King Hussein crushed the Fedayeen guerrillas in 1970. Voices have been heard in the Palestinian Liberation Organization (PLO) favoring establishment of a national authority on the West Bank and the Gaza Strip—a position incorporated into an official PLO policy-declaration in the summer of 1974. And after the Arab summit decision at Rabat later that year to vest in the PLO the sole right to represent the Palestinians, Jordan reluctantly veered from the dominant line of its policy since 1967. Previously it had insisted on reacquiring the West Bank, although in 1972 King Hussein held out the prospect that the territory would have greater autonomy than before 1967. The prospect of a third state, implicit in the Rabat decision, is nevertheless regarded as apprehensively by Jordan as by Israel. Something approaching an international consensus has evolved since the October, 1973, war in favor of a three-state solution that satisfies Palestinian political aspirations in an independent West Bank-Gaza Strip state, and that leaves intact the territorial integrity of Israel in roughly its pre-1967 borders and of Jordan without the West Bank. That such a solution finds no favor with officially stated Israeli policy, that it is the subject of open dissension among politically potent Palestinians and that it remains an outcome that Jordan does not favor—all suggest how great the distance is to peace through repartition.

And, finally, not everyone in a position to influence events agrees that the principle of territorial repartition has much relevance one way or the other. Former Israeli Defense Minister Moshe Dayan, who more than anyone else set the character of the Israeli occupation after 1967, favored a tighter integration of the life of the West Bank and the Gaza Strip with Israel. For him this meant an intermixing of populations and activities across newly-porous borders, including establishment of Israeli settlements in populated as well as unpopulated areas of the territories. He allowed West Bank residents to retain Jordanian citizenship, and he left most Jordanian law in force. His hope, however, was to create such a dense network of functional ties that issues of future sovereignty and precise political boundaries would become secondary. This basic conception guided his practical policies toward the occupied territories during his tenure, although the concept was never wholeheartedly implemented. While a policy of maximum integration—without formal annexation—did have selective strong support of leading figures in the governing coalition, it provoked vigorous objection from others in the leadership who believed that it would inevitably lead to *de facto* incorporation of an Arab population so large that it would undermine Israel's essential Jewish majority. Dayan's successor, Shimon Peres, has prominently urged federation between the two territories and Israel—on the ground that this is the only alternative to what he calls "an impossible partition."[3] As he put it to an American television audience in 1975: "When you have two people living on the very same land, you can either divide the land and have partition, or divide the government and have federation."[4] In elaborating his proposal elsewhere, he has said that a federal structure between Israel and the Palestinians in the territories would leave defense, foreign affairs, and financial decisions in the hands of the central government of Israel, while devolving to regional levels and to locally-elected Palestinian bodies responsibility for all other governmental functions.

Views about repartition are this wide-ranging and divisive because they connect with the deepest roots of the conflict between Israel and the Palestinians. What divides them are not just issues of real estate—although territorial questions are obviously involved. The political future of the West Bank and the Gaza Strip touches each party's core self-interests and self-conceptions, deriving from their historical experiences, from religious and cultural identifications, from the weight of an unsatisfactory *status quo,* and from apprehensions about a future that can be neither predicted nor guaranteed. To many Israelis, one observer writes, "If the location of the borders with Egypt and Syria involves largely issues of military security on the Israeli side and return of lost territory to the states concerned, the controversy over the Gaza Strip and the West Bank touches Israel's most sensitive nerve—the legitimacy of its statehood."[5] One of the country's leading intellectuals has explained that even those Israelis "who are not in favor of annexing the West Bank and Gaza Strip, and among those who know that the security problems may eventually be resolved, there is profound resistance to granting sovereign rights to the Palestinians in part of Palestine." He believes that such resistance "derives partly from the latent fear that recognition of the rights of Palestinians means, in itself, some measure of recognition of the justice of their arguments . . . and may, therefore, eventually imply a questioning of the very basis of Zionism."[6] To many Palestinians, likewise, the future of these territories, quite apart from reactions to the Israeli rule over them, touches their most sensitive nerve—the legitimacy of their struggle against Zionism in Palestine. Even the uncertain and hypothetical possibility in recent years that the territories might be traded for peace has triggered within the PLO and the Palestinian establishment a bitter internal debate about whether participation in any political process that regains only the West Bank and the Gaza Strip would be tantamount to a sellout—via a partition whose legitimacy has never had official Palestinian sanction and whose practical effect might be to put beyond reach the maximum political and military objectives against Israel.

The debate about repartition will be accelerated by any new efforts to move forward the Middle East peace negotiations that stalled after the Sinai II Pact between Israel and Egypt. For at some stage those negotiations will almost certainly bear on the political future of the West Bank and the Gaza Strip. There exists today a rhetorical consensus among Israel and Arabs that the Palestinian-Israeli dimension of the conflict must be dealt with in the context of a satisfactory peace settlement. It is a misleading consensus, however, because beneath it each side is offering possible solutions that the other regards as totally unacceptable as a basis even for negotiations, much less for an agreed settlement. Yet, however distant the prospect of a mutually acceptable negotiating framework, it clearly must include some arrangements whereby the Israelis and Palestinians can begin to coexist peacefully, can both enjoy physical security, can satisfy their essential political aspirations, and can look to a future of well-being and vitality. No such arrangement is any longer conceivable unless a mutually satisfactory future can be found for the West Bank and the Gaza Strip, for these two territories have become something of a symbol of the Israeli-Palestinian conflict in its contemporary setting.

Any decision to repartition the area in ways affecting the political status of the West Bank and the Gaza Strip, or to reject such repartition, will be a step with economic implications that no involved political leader can ignore. This is so even though the transcendent historical, ideological, political, and security concerns are and will remain at the forefront of the Israeli-Palestinian agenda. In view of the long history of illusions about "economic approaches to peace" in the Middle East, it is important to be emphatic about the secondary importance of economic interests here. For the Israelis and Palestinians in particular, the dynamics of their conflict has exposed the frailty of hopes that peace and reconciliation could be nurtured by economic interdependence, by the attraction of economic satisfactions, or by the threat of economic deprivation. Violence and enmity between them will not be foregone for economic reasons, and peaceful coexistence will not be sought for its economic promise. And because the issues that divide them are not economic in nature, no basic amelioration of their confrontation can be brought appreciably closer by primarily economic policies.

Nevertheless, the economic dimension of the present situation in the West Bank and the Gaza Strip will become an increasingly important factor in political calculations about the future of the territories if and when a process begins for shaping that future through negotiations.The Israeli occupation has created a new pattern of economic relationships among Israel, the West Bank, the Gaza Strip, and Jordan. Indeed, during the past nine years, the area's overall economic contours have been reshaped more dramatically than at any time since the 1948 war, after which separate sovereignties divided the former mandate region. Israelis and Palestinians—and this point cannot be overstressed—attach widely divergent interpretations to the new pattern, to its causes, its significance, and its bearing on prospects for peaceful accommodation. Whether this pattern of economic relationships should be maintained, severed, or reoriented in the future looms as an important question of basic interests for all who are directly involved in setting the political future of the West Bank and the Gaza Strip.

Dr. Van Arkadie's findings and judgments stand on their own, and need no supplementary interpretation in this introduction. But some general historical and political observations are necessary because the economic experience of the West Bank and the Gaza Strip under Israeli rule has become to some extent bound up with contending Israeli and Arab visions of the links between economics and politics and peace in the Middle East. It is helpful to have these visions in mind when reading Van Arkadie's profile of the existing situation, for they have been filtered into the very different Israeli and Palestinian perceptions of the meaning of the past nine years.

Abba Eban, as Israel's foreign minister, told the Geneva Peace Conference in December, 1973, that his government believed the ultimate guarantee of any peace agreement should be dense economic relations between Israelis and Arabs, similar to the post World War II Western European model. He was restating a theme habitually articulated by or on behalf of Israel since 1948, and by earlier Zionist spokesmen discussing Jewish-Arab co-operation in Mandate Palestine. Although the variations on the theme have been many and have been tailored to specific historical circumstances, they stretch back to Theodore Herzl's utopian political novel, *Altneuland,* which portrayed a Jewish-Arab commonwealth in Palestine where Jewish immigration would bring mutual prosperity. A later generation of Israelis who founded the state would envision Israeli technology, manufactures, and financial resources combining with Arab raw materials, foodstuffs, and vast markets to bring economic development to the Middle East. Today, with financial fortunes reversed and technological balances uncertain over the long run, the traditional vision persists as an anticipation that Israel would be an Arab trading partner and "the Singapore of the Middle East."

As consistently as this vision has been sketched by Israelis, Arabs have rejected it as a foundation for coexistence. As the Peel Commission noted long ago, Arabs during the mandate period, while in fact benefiting from Jewish economic activity, continued to regard these benefits as incidental to the persistence of the unresolved political problems. After 1948 the Arab boycott of Israel set the temper for a generation of economic warfare. Through the boycott they not only withheld the *de facto* recognition of Israel that would have been attendant on economic dealings with her, but they also protected themselves from unfavorable competition with a rapidly industrializing country having a far more advanced technological infrastructure, greater financial potential, higher productive capacity, and a more vigorous and promising overall level of economic performance.

Between 1948 and 1967 this Israeli conception of peace and this Arab rejection of it passed each other by. It was a dialogue of the deaf. The whole issue was academic in a Middle East beset by constant political tensions and sporadic war. But when Israel acquired the West Bank and the Gaza Strip in the Six Day War, the matter ceased to be academic. Between the Israeli economy and an Arab one, the seal was now broken on the economic boycott. An untested vision of technological-economic coexistence now came face to face with a concrete opportunity.

Every Israeli cabinet since 1967, while insisting that there will be no return to the June, 1967, borders, has decided not to decide the political future of the West Bank and the Gaza Strip. But government policy, including economic policy, was grounded in three understandings. Israel would not formally annex the territories. Israel would not withdraw from them. And Israel would not allow them to become a net budget burden.

Each of these imperatives meant something different for economic policy. The first meant that the territories could be neither treated as if they were fully part of the Israeli economy nor tied to that economy in such ways that would amount to overt "economic annexation." The second meant that Israel had to deal somehow with economic needs of the people in the territories; as long as Israel was holding them, it could not simply be indifferent to their welfare. The third meant that the extent of Israeli economic activities was limited by the finite revenues provided directly or indirectly by the territories themselves, and that this ledger of resources and expenditures—not some overall economic plan—determined the level of Israeli public investment in the territories' economic development.

A certain logic of improvization worked itself out in the economic policies that Israel followed in the West Bank and the Gaza Strip. While the result fell short of the "maximum-integration" school of thought within the Israeli leadership, Israel did not simply conduct a holding action either. Economic life in the territories and their economic connections to Israel and to Jordan bore the stamp of Israeli steering and interests. And throughout the years of the occupation, economic life on the West Bank and in the Gaza Strip has remained an inescapably political subject, because no feature of the economic picture can be fully divorced from the dominant political reality: the Israelis exercise dominion, and the Palestinians want that dominion to end. Through this prism each party angles its perceptions of the economic situation, particularly since economic policies have played such a conspicuous role in the strategy of Israel's rule.

Van Arkadie indicates why West Bank and Gaza Strip economic performance is susceptible to differing interpretations even in strictly economic terms, and he suggests why long-term economic implications are discernible only with many caveats and much speculation. Not surprisingly, therefore, Israelis and Palestinians can marshal divergent verdicts on the economic situation. To understate or underestimate the depth or the durability of this divergence would be dangerously shortsighted, for it reflects widely dissimilar expectations about what would be feasible and desirable in the future.

Here, for example, is a characterization of the economic situation by an Israeli economist and official, Arie Bregman, whose study bears the imprimatur of the Bank of Israel. His periodic assessments of the economic situation in the territories are the leading sources of readily available professional economic analysis of this subject:

> The outstanding feature of the economy of the administered areas in the period under review was its extremely rapid growth. Gross national product rose by an annual average of 18 percent at constant prices—probably one of the highest rates in the world, especially among developing countries. . . .
> These figures far exceed those from the pre-1967 period. . . .
> The rapid and continuous growth of the areas' economies must be attributed to the close ties established between them and the Israeli economy. The abrupt removal of the barriers that had separated the two economies' populations and prevented trade between them, created in fact a common market of three economies: those of Israel, the West Bank and the Gaza Strip.[7]

Israeli government publications not aimed at professional economists, as the Bank's reports are, call attention to the same result. A fact-book released in Israel just prior to the October, 1973, war sums up: "The years of Israeli administration have already produced the period of the greatest prosperity in the history of the West Bank and the Gaza Strip."[8] And almost three years later, the Israeli embassy in Washington released, in advance of the municipal elections on the West Bank, a policy paper proclaiming that "the economic progress that has been registered in the Israel-administered areas (an average annual growth of 18 percent in GNP), which is manifest everywhere, is a more powerful fact of life than all the propaganda of the PLO."[9]

At about the same time that this Bank of Israel study was released in Jerusalem, an economic and social history of the West Bank under both Jordanian and Israeli rule was published in Arabic by Jamil Hilal under the auspices of the Palestine Liberation Organization Research Center in Beirut. Hilal first argues that between 1948 and 1967 the West Bank economy was "suffocated" by Jordanian leaders primarily concerned about economic development of the East Bank—a conclusion shared, incidentally, by some Israeli analysts. Then he characterizes the post-1967 period this way:

> The West Bank—and also the Gaza Strip—has become an Israeli colony in all meanings of the word. The economy of the West Bank was tailored to suit the economic and capital investment requirements of Israel. The Israeli occupation has forced on the West Bank a type of dependent specialization. . . . Basically, the West Bank has come to trade with the Israeli economy, while its internal markets remained restrained, backward, and its economic activities lacked any form of cohesion. This can be explained . . . by the integration of the West Bank and the Israeli economies. . . .

"The Israeli control over the West Bank economy," he continues, "has produced several forms of exploitation, the most important of which are . . . monetary exploitation . . . trade exploitation . . . [and] exploitation of the labor force."[10]

These contrasting portrayals of prosperity versus exploitation draw upon many of the same "objective" facts. Van Arkadie's analysis, the Bregman study, and the Hilal book all suggest a "yes-and-no" answer to the question: Has Israel brought economic development to the West Bank and the Gaza Strip? With economic indicators pointing in both directions, a cumulative judgment depends ultimately on which qualitative economic criteria are applied to the evidence. The facts do not "speak for themselves." But whatever verdict is chosen, and however it is hedged, competing Israeli and Palestinian perspectives on the meaning of the economic situation remain as much a part of the local reality as GNP estimates, price and income data, and trends in agricultural or industrial productivity.

The above-quoted excerpt from the Bank of Israel study, even with its unemotional style, captures a sense of Israeli pride in their economic accomplishments. Israelis can point to upbeat economic trends. They can argue that despite existing political and security constraints they have raised the living standards of the Arab population. Simplistic ideas about peace growing out of economic coexistence may have attracted some Israeli adherents, but what prevailed—this certainly was the case with Dayan—was a more sober awareness of the practical dividends that a healthy economic environment would pay. Serious economic dislocation or deprivation after 1967 would have invited political unrest and given an incentive to active resistance. Economic collapse in the territories, whatever its adverse human and social effects, was simply not a tolerable or viable outcome for Israel. "Economic crisis is the fuel for any underground movement," one seasoned Israeli journalist and Dayan-watcher wrote in connection with Dayan's West Bank policy. Economic crisis was therefore to be avoided lest Israel "forfeit its military victory in the vegetable market."[11] In any event, although their reasons have varied, Israelis have tended to attach substantial significance to the economic features of their West Bank-Gaza Strip policies.

Most Palestinian viewpoints, however, have tended to downplay the significance of these same economic considerations. There is resistance, in particular, to drawing political conclusions from economic facts and to using economic rationales as an opening wedge for arguing that existing economic relations must determine the anatomy of future political relationships. Palestinians respond either by challenging the claims of economic advancement since 1967 or by asserting that the claims merely divert attention from what is regarded as the real issue of terminating Israeli rule. And even among the West Bank or Gaza Strip Palestinians who do not deny that Israeli rule has brought some economic benefits, the political factors are given precedence. Israelis expect this. The Israeli military governor for the two territories once told a Western journalist that West Bankers want "the benefits of Israel without Israel."[12]

These Israeli and Palestinian perceptions of the past nine years are tied to a subtle appreciation that the economic realities convey some very basic political intentions and convictions. Some Israelis saw their control over the West Bank and the Gaza Strip as an unprecedented crack in the Arab boycott. So they sought to widen this crack dramatically. The chief economic policy-planner in the West Bank military administration in the summer of 1967,

Baruch Yekutieli, who is reported to have given the name "open bridges" to the policy of allowing passage of goods and people across the Jordan River bridges, was zealously committed to this idea. "Through the West Bank," according to one Israeli account of his views, "he hoped to create economic, cultural and even political contacts with the Arab countries." When asked whether he thought encouragement of exports from the West Bank to the East Bank was worth it, he is reported to have answered: "Worth it? Export? Don't you realize where this could lead to? They are selling in the East Bank—that's export. They get money and can buy goods—that's import, that is to say credit. Credit means banks, agreements on both sides; agreements between banks are almost like agreements between governments, economic agreements. First, perhaps, clearing, then commercial agreements, perhaps delegations . . . don't you see how far things could go?" He is said to have reasoned that "it was highly unlikely that Israel would retain the West Bank forever. When finally forced to evacuate it, there would be a unique opportunity to make commercial contacts in the Arab world and to establish normal relations."[13]

While such unvarnished enthusiasm waned before long, there was no lessening of Israeli determination to maintain the newly-established economic interconnections if peace ever came. The West Bank and Gaza Strip economic experience was more and more often held up as the success story of the traditional vision of peaceful economic coexistence that Israelis have so frequently embraced. Arab interpreters have made plain their awareness that this line of thinking about the West Bank is taken seriously in Israel. One Egyptian intellectual has recently referred to the traditional wish of Israel's leaders to "use the economy to integrate themselves into the Middle East, which means they would set up a system of exchanges in which Israel would furnish the capital, the skill, and the manufactured products, while the Arab states, whose economic level was so much lower, would furnish raw materials, agricultural products, and possibly labor. In short, the same thing would happen that is happening now on the West Bank." He added that Israeli leaders, aware of their natural economic advantages in this situation, realize "the organic importance of exchanges between Israel and the West Bank. In all their statements concerning the Arab-Israeli negotiations, they emphasize the need to open the economic frontiers on both sides."[14]

And indeed Israeli officials have been clear about this. The first military governor of the West Bank, Chaim Herzog, now Israel's ambassador to the United Nations, stressed in 1970 that even if the road to overall Arab-Israeli peace is long, he believed that the "direction toward solution lies in developments in the occupied areas." "We have finally arrived at a situation," he pointed out, "in which a definite flow of commerce crosses over from the areas under Israeli control to the Arab world and back again, and from Israel itself, too, although I will not say much more about that aspect of it." He projected that "whatever the agreement . . . it will include the principle of open borders—at least as open as they are today, if not more so."[15]

Over the period of Israeli rule, Van Arkadie's study shows, the extent of trading interconnections over the open bridges has remained modest, even declining in relative economic significance before 1967; and the Israelis have not encouraged large-scale imports into the West Bank from the Arab world. But it is not the quantity that matters. Symbolically, even the limited and essentially one-way economic trade-flows strike a vital political chord in Israel. Not only, the Israelis say, must peace bring open trade in principle with the Arab world at-large, the barriers that came down in 1967 also must not again be rebuilt. Israeli cabinet minister Chaim Bar-Lev, for example, said in 1974 that the West Bank and Israel are now and will remain one economic unit no matter what the political settlement in the region will be.[16]

One Palestinian response, which is a logical extension of the prosperity versus exploitation themes, is to deny in principle that the West Bank experience constitutes a successful long-term antidote to the Arab boycott. Not only, Hilal writes, have the open bridges worked to preserve Jordanian influence in the West Bank, but they have also given Israel a basis for its hoped-for "great movement of persons and goods between Israel and other parts of the Arab countries." Hilal argues for removal of what are regarded as the inequities of the existing Israeli-Palestinian economic relationship. Israeli-sponsored economic development in the two territories, he observes, "is in line with Israeli vision and thinking for a political settlement in the area, the main condition of which is the dissolution of the Arab boycott and, significantly, the establishment of economic and trade relations with the Arab countries." The economic pattern evolving under Israeli rules, he asserts,

> creates strong fears that the occupied areas, especially the West Bank, will play the role of 'the intermediate colony' between Israel and the Arab markets in case of a political settle-

ment in the future. These fears will not be alleviated by an Israeli military withdrawal from these occupied areas if this withdrawal is not accompanied by an end to imperialist economic and trade relations that currently exist. The economic dependence of the West Bank on the Israeli economy that was brought about by the Israeli occupation forces must be cancelled, while at the same time there should be a complete and dynamic growth in the industrial base of the West Bank and the Gaza Strip without any dependence on the economic and political aspects of the Israeli economy—that is, the creation of a truly national economy in the occupied areas.[17]

Van Arkadie's study does not try to judge whether these sharply contrasting approaches to the economic future of the West Bank and the Gaza Strip can be reconciled. Not only is the question beyond his mandate, it is also beyond the boundaries of economic analysis, *per se*. What he does try to provide, however, is a general profile of the economic links that today connect the economies of Israel, the West Bank, the Gaza Strip, and Jordan. On the basis of this profile, he offers a preliminary appraisal of economic interests that seem most likely to come into play in any decisions bearing on the political future of the two territories controlled by Israel since 1967.

Footnotes

1. Neguib Azoury, *Le Réveil de la Nation Arabe dans l'Asie Turque en Présence des Intérêts et des Rivalités des Puissances Etrangères* (Paris, 1905), p. 48.

2. Palestine Royal Commission, *Report Cmd. 5479* (London: H.M. Stationery Office, 1937), pp. 370 and 371.

3. *Jerusalem Post,* April 25, 1975.

4. CBS Television, *Face the Nation,* December 14, 1975.

5. Abraham S. Becker, *Israel and the Palestinian Occupied Territories: Military-Political Issues in the Debate* (Santa Monica, California: The Rand Corporation, 1971), p. iii.

6. Saul Friedlander in Friedlander and Mahmoud Hussein, *Arabs and Israelis: A Dialogue* (New York: Holmes and Meier, 1975), pp. 215-216.

7. Arie Bregman, *Economic Growth in the Administered Areas, 1968-1973* (Jerusalem: Bank of Israel Research Department, 1975), p. 4.

8. *Information Briefing 28: Facts about the Administered Areas* (Jerusalem: Israel Information Centre, n.d.), p. 24.

9. *Information Background: The Spring 1976 Municipal Elections in Judaea and Samaria* (Washington, D.C.: Embassy of Israel, n.d.), pp. 4-5.

10. Jamil Hilal, *The West Bank: Its Social and Economic Structure (1948-1974)* (Beirut: Palestine Liberation Organization Research Center, 1975), pp. 284-286. (Original in Arabic.)

11. Shabtai Teveth, *The Cursed Blessing: The Story of Israel's Occupation of the West Bank* (London: Weidenfeld and Nicolson, 1969), p. 95.

12. John M. Goshko, "The West Bank: Going It Alone," *Washington Post,* June 1, 1975.

13. See Teveth, *op. cit.* pp. 144-145, 146, 149-150. Technical-level discussions between Israelis and Jordanians were so ambitious at one point, that they apparently exceeded the political tolerances of the Israeli political leadership. One account claims that representatives of Israeli and Jordanian banks, after meeting with the military government on the West Bank, initialed an agreement by which imported Arab oil would be refined at Haifa, and Haifa would be used as a point of trans-shipment of goods for Jordan and possibly ultimately to other Arab countries. The agreement was scrapped by the Minister of Justice (Pinhas Sapir) and Prime Minister Levi Eshkol, who reportedly preferred to wait for government-to-government agreements after an expected early peace with Jordan. See "Israel and the Palestinians: A Discussion" in Shlomo Avineri, ed., *Israel and the Palestinians* (New York: St. Martin's Press, 1971), pp. 122-123.

14. Mahmoud Hussein in Friedlander and Hussein, *op. cit.,* pp. 10, 191.

15. Quoted in "Israel and the Palestinians: A Discussion" in Avineri, ed., *op. cit.,* pp. 119-120.

16. *Jerusalem Post,* July 9, 1974.

17. Hilal, *op. cit.,* pp. 233, 267-68.

Chapter 1

Historical Background

The Middle East wars of 1948 and 1967 not only altered political boundaries, they also led to major changes in patterns of regional economic activity. In particular, these two wars were decisive turning points in the economic history of the West Bank and the Gaza Strip.

Before 1948, when the two territories were part of the British Mandate for Palestine, connections between the economic life of the Jewish and Arab populations were limited in many important respects, but some elements of an all-Palestine economy had begun to take shape.[1] These early tendencies toward a unified economy during the mandate period were the background against which the architects of the 1947 U.N. Partition Plan could propose that the new Jewish and Arab States be linked by economic union and common economic planning institutions. This proposed framework, outlined in the General Assembly's Partition Resolution, seems utopian in restrospect. At the time, however, it did reflect an important aspect of pre-1948 economic reality. The economy of the Palestine Mandate had contained many elements of an integrated system, including a network of transport and other services, growing internal trade, a common currency, and a common tax system. During the mandate years, moreover, Jerusalem played an important role in the economic life of both Palestine and Transjordan, and Palestine was Transjordan's main transit route for international trade.

After 1948 these economic links were severed. For the next nineteen years, there was total isolation between the Israeli economy and the economies of the West Bank and the Gaza Strip. The West Bank became a part of Jordan and partially integrated into its economy. Although the Gaza Strip was administered by Egypt, it did not become economically integrated into Egyptian economic life. With the establishment of Israeli military rule over the two territories in 1967, the three economies once again came under the control of a single political authority, and the Israeli military administration in the West Bank and the Gaza Strip became directly responsible for the economic life of these areas and their relationships with neighboring economies.

Although this report surveys economic developments primarily since 1967, a brief review of the economic situation before 1967 is necessary to place the subsequent analysis in context.

DEVELOPMENTS BETWEEN 1948-67

The West Bank

The West Bank is the larger and more economically important of the two territories. Occupying an area of 2,165 square miles in the semi-arid hills west of the Jordan River, the West Bank had not been as intensely developed as the coastal regions of Mandate Palestine. With a 1946-47 Palestinian Arab population of 450,000, the West Bank was densely populated—over 200 persons per square mile. In the mandate period, the area later known as the West Bank did not attract large numbers of Jewish immigrants. The only city was Jerusalem—divided into Israeli and Arab sectors after 1948—which had a Palestinian Arab population of 60,000 in 1946-47. Important market towns then included Hebron (population, 24,000), Nablus (23,000), Bethlehem (8,500), Tulkarm (8,000) and Ramallah (5,000). During 1948 about 400,000 Arabs fled to the West Bank as refugees from parts of Palestine which were incorporated within Israel. Thousands of refugees relocated later to Jordan on the East Bank, thereby easing considerably the pressure of the West Bank's population growth. Additionally, a steady emigration to the Persian Gulf area slowed population growth after 1948 so that on the eve of the 1967 war the estimated population of the West Bank was 900,000.

Agricultural output was quite diversified, the most important crops being wheat, barley, lentils, olives and citrus fruits. However, due to the scarcity of water, only 35 percent of the total land was cultivated. Although irrigation was not widely practiced during the mandate period, there had been some successful experimentation with the irrigated cultivation of bananas and other crops in the narrow, below-sea-level valley adjacent to the Jordan River. The towns were mostly trade centers, the largest of them having important craft industries such as glass works in Hebron, embroidery in Bethlehem, and olive presses in Nablus, as well as some light manufacturing, including matches, textiles and soap.

The economic consequences of the 1948 war were severe for the West Bank. It lost its primary domestic market and source of supply for a wide range of products. It lost access to Haifa and other Mediterranean ports. Its transportation and communications systems, based upon the all-Palestine network, lost much of their practicality. Thousands of inhabitants lost their jobs in cities that became part of Israel, and hundreds of villagers lost productive land which remained on the opposite side of the 1949 armistice line. In addition, an influx of Arab refugees from Israel doubled the West Bank's population and further strained its already disrupted economy.[2]

The political realities of 1948 forced a complete reorientation of the West Bank's economic relationships. Surrounded by Israel on the north, west, and south, its only Arab neighbor was the desert kingdom of Transjordan on the East Bank. In 1948 the population of Transjordan was 350,000-400,000 consisting chiefly of Bedouin pastoralists whose few permanent agricultural villages were in the hills overlooking the Jordan Valley. The economy of Transjordan had virtually no industry and only limited agricultural development. During the mandate, Transjordan had been an economic satellite of Palestine, which consumed or trans-shipped most of the East Bank's meager exports. Amman had developed into a large town primarily due to its position as the administrative center for the country. Economic connections existed less between the West Bank and Transjordan than between both of them and the coastal areas of Palestine, on which both were dependent for their external communications and which comprised Israel after 1948.[3]

The reoriented economic relationships left the West Bank inevitably and increasingly dependent on Transjordan. Only through it could all economic transactions with the rest of the world take place. Dependence was reinforced in 1950 when the Hashemite kingdom formally annexed the area, making the comparatively advanced West Bank not only a part of a larger state, but also combining it with a less developed region with which previously it had had little significant economic connection.

Despite the West Bank's lack of natural resources, limited agricultural potential, undeveloped industrial base, and the presence of a destitute refugee population, it benefited to some extent from the Jordanian economy's high rate of economic growth, which averaged 10 percent per annum between 1950 and 1967.[4] Per capita income per annum rose from $90 to $200. A modest growth of industry involved the manufacture of consumer goods in East Jerusalem, Nablus, Hebron, Bethlehem, and Ramallah. Agricultural production was raised through investment and improved techniques. United Nations assistance eased the plight of the Palestinian refugees.

Nevertheless, the West Bank still had unresolved economic problems. There was a high rate of open unemployment. The West Bank's economy remained based largely upon agriculture, which provided jobs for almost one-half of the labor force of 150,000. However, this agricultural work force was underemployed. Since virtually all the land which was cultivable with existing irrigation facilities was already being farmed in 1948, it had not been possible to absorb the refugees in agriculture. Moreover, the location of jobs, the establishment of factories, and the development of other urban occupations barely kept pace with natural population growth. Urban growth in Jordan had been concentrated in the capital city of Amman. The West Bank's unemployment level was not worse only because thousands of refugees, as well as native West Bankers, migrated to find work in the East Bank, the Persian Gulf area, and farther afield. Income from labor in the East Bank and from remittances of West Bankers abroad became an important source of income growth. Table I-1 indicates that remittances totaled 6.4 million dinars, or 11.8 percent of the West Bank's gross domestic product.[5]

To go beyond this rather general description of the economy of the West Bank during this period to a more precise assessment is difficult because available data are inadequate. It is particularly difficult to quantify the extent of the economic interconnections that developed between the East and West Banks. Because the two regions were politically a single unit, most data were published on a unified basis, distinguishing neither the separate contributions of the two regions to the national product, nor the economic exchanges between them.

Table I-1

Balance of Payments for the West Bank, 1965

(In Thousands of Dinars)

	Credit	Debit	Net
Current Account	13,329	24,882	−11,553
Goods*	1,937	23,595**	−21,658
Services	11,392	1,287	10,105
Jordanian Government	11,151	11,151	
Purchases in West Bank	9,303		9,303
Current payments to households	265		265
Debit balance of local authorities in West Bank	183		183
Jordanian income from West Bank (taxes, etc.)		8,511	− 8,511
Posting and finance accounts	1,400		1,400
Net government capital account		2,640	− 2,640
Transfer Payments	10,045		10,045
From Jordanians abroad	6,398		6,398
From Ministry of Social Welfare and Employment	3,647		3,647
Capital Movements, Net Errors and Omissions	1,508		1,508
Total	36,033	36,033	

*Imported goods are CIF values (cost, insurance and freight charges included) exported goods are FOB values (free on board).

**The composition of imports:

Consumption goods	15,459
Intermediate goods	7,322
Capital goods	814
Total	23,595

NOTE: This and the subsequent tables in this chapter are presented in the original currencies, as calculated by the Economic Planning Authority. The official exchange rate of the dinar, the Egyptian pound, and the Israeli pound to the dollar in the period 1962 to the third quarter of 1967 was: Israeli pound = $3.00, Egyptian pound = $2.30, and Jordanian dinar = $2.80. By the fourth quarter of 1967, the Israel pound was devalued to 3.50 to the dollar. These figures have not been translated into the same unit; to do so might suggest an exact comparability which would not be justified. The problem of comparing pre- and post-1967 income and output levels is discussed in Chapter VI.

SOURCE: Economic Planning Authority,
   Economic Survey of the West Bank
   (Jerusalem:1967), Table 4, p. 21.

When the West Bank changed hands in 1967, the Israeli military authorities conducted an economic survey of the territory, using available Jordanian data.[6] In Chapter VI of this study, an assessment is given of the degree to which these early Israeli estimates can be used as a baseline for judging subsequent developments; no one would claim very high reliability for them, given the weaknesses typical of the underlying data in a poor economy and the difficulty of compiling a survey in immediate postwar conditions. Therefore, the figures given here regarding the structure of the West Bank economy at that time have to be treated with some caution. Nevertheless, the picture that emerges is plausible enough.

The sectoral distribution of gross domestic product, shown in Table I-2, is in most respects what would be expected for an economy at that level of development. The contribution of industry is small, accounting for less than 7 percent of output, while agriculture accounts for 24 percent. The heavy preponderance of the service sector is more unusual.

The relative importance of the service sector is probably explained by a number of factors illustrated by the balance of payments figures set out in Table I-1. Services generated the major credit item in the current account, largely through the income from tourism. The West Bank was the center of the Jordanian tourist trade, not only because overseas tourists were attracted to Jerusalem and other religious sites, but also because Middle Eastern tourists were attracted by the climate and pleasant environment of such places as Ramallah. Tourist income plus a combination of governmental subventions (including United Nations Relief and Works Agency [UNRWA]), capital inflows, and private transfers enabled the economy to maintain a large deficit in commodity trade. The Jordanian balance of payments was supported by substantial aid flows in this period. This meant that the West Bank—and, indeed, Jordan as a whole—was able to consume far more commodities than were produced locally. The result was a relatively large service sector and much smaller contribution of commodity production to gross domestic product than is typical for an economy at that income level.

The figures in Tables I-1 and I-2 suggest that before 1967 the most important external economic connections of the West Bank economy were through services, in particular tourism; public financial transfers (including UNRWA); and private transfers, resulting from residents working outside the region. Commodity

Table I-2

Gross Domestic Product by Sectors in the West Bank, 1965

Sector	Thousands of dinars	Percent	Percent of West Bank contribution to GNP of Jordan
Agriculture	12,998	23.9	38
Industry	3,576	6.6	26
Quarrying*	646	1.2	26
Construction	3,147	5.8	40
Electricity and water	587	1.1	35
Transportation	3,229	5.9	26
Trade	12,574	23.1	40
Banking and finance	844	1.5	40
Home ownership	4,276	7.8	40
Public services and security	7,492	13.7	35
Other services	5,132	9.4	40
Total	54,501	100.0	36

*Stone quarries.

SOURCE: *Economic Survey of the West Bank,* Table 1, p. 9.

exports were a relatively minor factor in the balance of payments and, *a fortiori,* an even less important part of total product.

Exports from the West Bank were estimated to be only 1.9 million dinars, compared to a gross domestic product of 54.5 million dinars. These exports derived from fruit, quarry, and olive oil production. Agricultural exports accounted for under 11 percent of the sales of agriculture and the food processing industries.[7] (West Bank income data are summarized in Tables I-3 and I-4.)

The more subtle aspects of economic interconnections between the East and West Banks are not demonstrated by an analysis of trade flows. Any underdeveloped economy having a large agricultural sector in part producing for subsistence and depending heavily on imports for manufactured goods, will show a very simple pattern of inter-industry connections; that is, there will only be limited trading links between different domestic industries. East Bank-West Bank interconnections were typical of this pattern. However, the web of private financial links and the

Table I-3

Sources and Uses of Income in the West Bank —1965

(Thousands of Dinars)

Sources		Uses	
Gross Domestic Product (GDP) at Market Prices		Private Uses	54,779
		Local Authorities	
Factor cost)*	54,501	Jordanian govern-	
Indirect taxes	2,986	ment	700
		Other	9,303
Total	57,487	Total	10,003
Imports			
Goods	23,595	Capital Flow	8,650
Services	1,287	Exports	
Import duties	4,392	Exported goods	1,937
		Exported services	11,392
Total	29,274	Total	13,329
Total Sources:	86,761		
		Total Uses	86,761

*Income of Jordanian citizens abroad is not included in this total.

SOURCE: *The Economy of the West Bank (1967).*
Table II, p.20—(Hebrew original)

movement of labor may very well have been more complex. For it is evident that after 1948, as the East Bank developed and Amman grew from being a small town into a city, the Palestinian population of the East Bank grew. Not only were there Palestinian workers on the East Bank, but many Palestinian families developed an economic stake on both sides of the Jordan River.

The Gaza Strip

The 1948 war created for the Gaza Strip problems even greater than those of the West Bank. During the mandate, the town of Gaza, with a population of approximately 40,000, had been a significant commercial center and port, serving the area south of Tel Aviv-Jaffa and the Hebron and Beersheba districts. The harbor handled a modest volume of export-import trade, the town's

Table I-4

Sources of West Bank Income, 1965
(In Thousands of Dinars)

a.	Gross domestic product (at factor cost)	54,501
b.	Less depreciation	2,254
c.	Net domestic product	52,247
d.	Payments from the public sector	360
e.	Remittances from Jordanian citizens abroad	6,398
f.	Payments from the ministry of welfare and employment and other institutions	3,647
g.	Indirect taxes	— 775
h.	Payments to the public sector	— 1,634
i.	Private income (c + d + e + f—g—h)	60,243
j.	Population (in thousands)	900
k.	Private income per capita (in dinars) (i ÷ j)	66.9

SOURCE: *The Economy of the West Bank,* Table III, p. 20.

wholesale and retail markets played an important part in the country's agricultural marketing system, and a number of workshops flourished, including such traditional crafts as pottery and weaving.

During the 1948 war, Gaza was occupied by the Egyptian army and cut off from its natural hinterland, which became part of Israel. The area under Egyptian administration until 1967— except for a brief interlude after the 1956 Suez War—totaled only 140 square miles. This area, which became known as the Gaza Strip, included the town of Gaza, one other small town, eight farming villages, and a few Bedouin encampments. The pre-1948 population had been roughly 60,000.

Cut off from its hinterland, separated from Egypt by the barren, largely uninhabited Sinai Peninsula, and lacking natural resources except underground water supplies, the Gaza Strip was forced to reorient its economy under the most unfavorable conditions. An additional factor of serious economic consequence was the presence of Arab refugees from what had been southern Palestine. In 1948-49, about 150,000 people fled to the strip, tripling the population just when the basis for local economic activity had been undermined. The United Nations through UNRWA soon assumed responsibility for the refugees and eventually established eight large, semi-permanent camps for their housing. However, given the general inability of the local economy to absorb them in productive employment, the situation of the refugees remained grim, at best, and they failed to experience even the limited improvement in living standards enjoyed by some refugees on the West Bank. The high rate of natural increase among both the original population and refugees aggravated conditions further. By 1967 the total population was nearly 400,000. Emigration was not as important as in the West Bank, and consequently remittances sent back to Gaza families were less extensive.

The primary basis of the Gaza Strip economy between 1948 and 1967 was agriculture. Table I-5 shows the industrial composition of the gross domestic product (GDP) of the Gaza Strip in 1966. Agriculture accounted for one-third of all employment and production and for more than 90 percent of all exports. Citrus fruits comprised the most important crop and were the main foreign exchange earner. Eastern Europe and England were the principal markets for Gaza's citrus exports. Dates also were exported but were insignificant in comparison to citrus fruits. Other crops included barley, wheat, melons, and vegetables, but their production was insufficient to meet local demand. Milk, poultry, and fish production generally was adequate to satisfy local consumption, but processed dairy products and meat had to be imported. Gaza Strip agriculture, with its water sources scarce and its soil increasingly saline, had reached by 1967 the limits of its potential with existing farming methods.

In their contribution to the Gaza Strip economy, trade and services ranked second to agriculture on the eve of the Israeli occupation. A special feature of the strip's commerce was the development of an entrepôt and smuggling trade with Egypt. Since the average level of customs duties in the strip was very low in comparison with those prevailing in Egypt, imported goods, especially luxury items, were generally inexpensive. This encouraged an influx, during the 1960s, of Egyptian tourist-shoppers in the Gaza Strip, whose merchants also found lucrative opportunities to smuggle imports into Egypt. Available data do not indicate the share of Gaza Strip imports destined for re-export via tourist sales and smuggling, but most observers believe it to have been as high as two-thirds.[8]

Other circumstances also led to the development of an extensive service sector in the Gaza Strip. The Egyptian army main-

Table I-5

The Gaza Strip: Sources of Income, 1966

	Millions of Egyptian pounds	Percent
Gross Domestic Output by Sector		
Agriculture and fishing	5.5	26.2
Industry	0.7	3.3
Trade and personal services*	4.3	20.5
Transport	0.5	2.4
Administration and public services**	4.0	19.0
Building and public construction	1.0	4.8
Total	16.0	76.2
Transfers from Abroad		
UNRWA and other public transfers	4.0	19.0
Remittances from relatives abroad	1.0	4.8
Total	5.0	23.8
Total Income from All Sources	21.0	100.0

*Services include banking and insurance; house rents are not included in this table.

**Including the activities of the Palestinian Liberation Army.

SOURCE: Economic Planning Authority, *The Economy of the Gaza Strip and Sinai* (Jerusalem: Central Bureau of Statistics, 1967), Table 6, p. 8.

tained an adjacent base, while after 1964 the Palestine Liberation army operated in the Strip. Soldiers of the U.N. Emergency Forces also were based there, and UNRWA employed a large staff to run its camps, schools, and medical clinics. The presence of all these military and civilian personnel encouraged the proliferation of personal service occupations.

In contrast to the other economic sectors, industry in the Gaza Strip was undeveloped, consisting almost exclusively of small workshops. Weaving of textiles and carpets comprised the most important manufacturing enterprise. Non-traditional business up to 1967 included beverage bottling plants and citrus packing houses. Unemployment and underemployment were high. Annual per capita income, which did not exceed $125 in 1967, was lower than in the West Bank.

THE AFTERMATH OF THE 1967 WAR

As in 1948, the 1967 war brought severe economic disruption to the West Bank and the Gaza Strip, fundamentally altering settled economic relationships to neighboring economies.

In the Gaza Strip, tourist trade from Egypt disappeared, adversely affecting the trade, service and handicrafts sectors dependent upon it. Local income derived from servicing Egyptian, United Nations, and local military forces was eliminated. The repercussions included severe unemployment and closure of workshops and stores. There was some emigration following the 1967 war, but not as large as from the West Bank. The general economic stagnation increased the already-serious economic difficulties of the 356,000 Palestinians who remained in the densely overpopulated strip, 75 percent of whom were concentrated in towns and refugee camps of at least 10,000 or more, and about one-fourth (118,000) of whom lived in Gaza City, including 30,000 in the adjacent Gaza Beach refugee camp.

The economic situation in the West Bank was also serious. During and immediately after the war some 200,000 Palestinians—one-quarter of the total population—fled to the East Bank. These included thousands of refugees who had been receiving remittances in hard currency from abroad and many skilled workers in the small labor force. This significant population loss adversely affected many sectors of the economy. Agriculture was least affected—except in the Jordan Valley—as families stayed with their land. Banks, whose funds had been transferred to Amman, were closed, disrupting businesses requiring banking services. By September, 1967, when 660,000 Palestinians remained in the West Bank and East Jerusalem, emigration to the East Bank began to slow down considerably. The major urban concentrations were East Jerusalem (65,000), Nablus (44,000), Hebron (38,000), Bethlehem and its suburbs (20,000), Ramallah-El Bireh (25,000), Tulkarm (15,000) and Jenin (13,000). In all, approximately 46 percent of the population was urban, living in towns with 5,000 or more residents.

Among the early basic decisions that the Israeli government adopted, three have significantly shaped subsequent economic developments: the annexation of Arab East Jerusalem, the encouragement of "open bridges" between the West and East Banks, and the institution of "open borders" between Israel and the two territories of the West Bank and the Gaza Strip.

The annexation of the former Jordanian sector of Jerusalem in the summer of 1967 sought to incorporate the West Bank's largest city and its most important commercial center into Israel in all senses, including economic. The immediate economic effect was to change the fiscal status of the Palestinian residents, who became subject to Israeli taxes and economic administration. Nevertheless, the Jerusalem Palestinians have not been economically isolated from the rest of the West Bank. Businesses and families have maintained their economic links and have continued to do business not only with the rest of the West Bank but also with the East Bank.

Since 1967, economic data on East Jerusalem have been included in Israeli economic statistics neither included in data for the West Bank nor separately identifiable. The absence of such information causes a significant but unavoidable gap in this study, for there is no way of documenting the continuing connections with the West Bank, the impact of the shift in tourist business away from Arab Jerusalem, or other important features of the economic life of East Jerusalem since 1967.

The Israeli decision to maintain the Jordan River bridges selectively open for trade between the West and East Banks had as its principal economic motive the need to ensure a market for West Bank agricultural produce. The Israeli occupation began almost simultaneously with the summer harvest season. Since the West Bank agricultural surpluses tended to be similar to those of Israeli farms, it was feared that entry of West Bank produce into Israel would force prices lower than Israeli policymakers, responsive to domestic agricultural interests, would judge acceptable. For the Jordanians, continued imports from the West Bank provided foods which otherwise would have had to be imported from elsewhere, plus some produce for export, such as olive oil. These were the economic considerations that prompted both Israel and Jordan to permit agricultural trade to resume between the two banks. This trade included trans-shipment of Gaza citrus to the East Bank and other Arab markets. The movement of agricultural goods was substantially restored, but trade in industrial goods was more seriously disrupted.

Initially, Israel levied custom duties on all goods imported by the West Bank from the East Bank. In 1968, however, duty-free imports were allowed for some agricultural goods including wheat and barley (produced on the East Bank) and nuts and spices (from other Arab countries). Licenses and duties remained for other goods. Jordan initially permitted the import of industrial products from the West Bank. But as West Bank industries shifted to Israeli sources of supply, it became difficult to tell whether goods originated in Israel or the West Bank. So Jordan, in compliance with Arab boycott prohibitions on trade with Israel, placed increasing restrictions on industrial imports from the West Bank.

The open bridges policy has had another important consequence in facilitating the maintenance of a complex network of monetary and fiscal connections between the West and East Banks. While only Israeli pounds circulate in the Gaza Strip, the Jordanian dinar has continued to circulate alongside the Israeli pound as a legal currency on the West Bank. In fiscal terms the exact degree of the continuing connection is difficult to specify. The Jordanian government has continued to pay many of its former officials on the West Bank and has periodically made loans available to West Bank municipalities.

The third major economic decision taken by Israel in the years after 1967 was to promote selectively economic links between the two territories and Israel. This proved to be the decision having the greatest impact on the West Bank and the Gaza Strip economies. In 1968, steps were begun to link up the transportation, communications and utilities infrastructures of the West Bank and the Gaza Strip with those of Israel. In that same year, the Israeli government began issuing labor cards to permit Palestinians from the territories to work in Israel, commuting daily from their normal places of residence. Israeli businesses were granted permission to place subcontracting work (primarily for textiles) with firms and individuals in the West Bank and the Gaza Strip.

In the first year of occupation the most important flow of commodities from the West Bank and the Gaza Strip into Israel was generated by the widespread purchase of goods by individual Israelis visiting the territories, in many cases gaining access to a range of Arab artifacts and other commodities not previously readily available in Israel. Controls were initially applied to the movement of agricultural produce into Israel to protect Israeli agriculture, an interest that has continued to determine the movement of West Bank agricultural exports to Israel, the level of which grew in later years, on a selective basis. The markets of the

West Bank and Gaza Strip also were opened to the sale of Israeli products, while the Israeli external tariff was applied to overseas imports reaching the territories.

As a result of these three basic decisions, a new set of interconnections has developed between the West Bank and Gaza Strip and Israel. And a much modified pattern of economic links continued between the territories, particularly the West Bank, and the Jordanian economy. These new patterns evolved in some ways in response to strong market forces. But Israeli policy encouraged these forces to work without constraint in some economic sectors, and discouraged them in others.

Footnotes

1. For a detailed study of the Palestine Mandate's economy, see Said Himadeh, ed., *Economic Organization of Palestine* (Beirut: American University of Beirut, 1938).

2. The economic impact of the refugee influx is examined in Jamil Hilal, *The West Bank: Its Social and Economic Structure, 1948-1973* (Beirut: Palestine Liberation Organization Research Center, 1975), pp. 15-43. (Original in Arabic.)

3. Michael P. Mazur, "Economic Development of Jordan" in Charles A. Cooper and Sidney Alexander, eds., *Economic Development and Population Growth in the Middle East* (New York: American Elsevier, 1972), p. 211.

4. For a detailed discussion of Jordan's economic growth prior to 1967 see *ibid.,* pp. 214-230.

5. Economic Planning Authority, *Economic Survey of the West Bank* (Jerusalem: Central Bureau of Statistics, 1967), p. 12. (Original in Hebrew.)

6. *Ibid., passim.*

7. This probably is an underestimate in that it only accounts for major trading items, neglecting minor trade across the Jordan in other agricultural products and the products of the small industrial crafts sectors.

8. Arie Bregman, *Economic Growth in the Administered Areas, 1968-1973* (Jerusalem: Bank of Israel Research Department, 1975), p. 82.

Chapter 2

An Economic Perspective on the 1967-75 Period

In 1967 the Israeli government did not conceive or attempt to implement any systematic, large-scale plan to alter the economic structure of the West Bank and the Gaza Strip—although the annexation of Jerusalem carried with it inescapable and major economic implications. Nor was there an Israeli master-plan for changing the external economic relationships of the two occupied territories or a long-range vision of a preferred economic future for them. This was the case even though some changes were both large and inevitable under the prevailing political circumstances—for example, the severance of the Gaza Strip's economic connections with Egypt and with most of the territory's other main pre-1967 trading partners. For the West Bank and the Gaza Strip economies, however, what happened after 1967 was more complex and no less profound than if such a master-plan had actually existed.

Decisions initially taken to revive economic activity in the immediate postwar period were responses to the pressing and immediate need for some sort of normalcy. Subsequent Israeli economic policy was responsive to various other influences—the requirements of the Israeli economy, economic opportunities provided by access to the two territories, the political or security considerations that shaped Israel's overall policy toward the territories, and the divisions of opinion within the Israeli leadership about the future of these areas.[1]

The most crucial of these initial policy decisions were those identified at the end of the previous chapter: to allow and then to encourage employment of Arab labor from the territories in the Israeli economy; to open the markets of the territories to the inflow of Israeli products; and to allow the sale in Israel of goods from the territories, first in a limited and controlled fashion, subsequently more freely but still with selective controls. The practical effect of these decisions was to expose the economies of the West Bank and the Gaza Strip to powerful market forces resulting from the differences in wage levels and economic structure between the territories and Israel, forces which acted mainly through the labor market and the commodity market.

Seen from this viewpoint, the pace and direction of economic changes that have occurred since 1967 resulted from decisions to unleash, promote, and mold these market forces—not under conditions of *laissez-faire,* but under the influence of overriding public policy considerations in both Israel and Jordan. Israel channeled and controlled the basic market forces while, at the same time, limiting severely the role of public investment and comprehensive development programs in the territories. Political and business factors, furthermore, operated to limit Israeli private investment in the territories. Jordan set policies aimed at protecting its own economic self-interest, and Jordan enforced Arab boycott policies aimed at preventing commercial contact between Israel and the Arab world. Israel imposed trade restrictions across the nominally "open" Jordan River bridges.[2] On the other hand, Israel allowed the continuation of Jordanian monetary and fiscal ties to the West Bank. All these factors, in combination with Jordanian policies, have regulated the economic environment throughout the period of Israeli rule over the West Bank and the Gaza Strip.

The most important economic effects of Israel's rule derived from the new linkages between the two territories and the Israeli economy, with its very different economic characteristics. In 1967-68, for example, per capita product in Israel was estimated to be ten times greater than that of the West Bank. Israel had benefited over the previous two decades from an injection of large amounts of capital, one of the factors resulting in a very high rate of growth in national product. Although experiencing a sharp recession in the years 1966 and 1967, the Israeli economy, after the

1967 war, entered a further period of boom that continued until 1974. The level of unemployment fell from the recession level of 10.4 percent in 1967, to 4.5 percent in 1969, to less than 3.0 percent in 1972 and 1973, and the boom created scarcity conditions in the Israeli labor market.

During the 1950s and 1960s not only had total output grown, but the structure of the Israeli economy also had been transformed. Agriculture had become more and more technically sophisticated and capital-intensive. Israel's large, complex, and highly protected industrial sector produced a wide range of manufactures. By 1959, industrial and construction activities accounted for more than one-third of the net national product, while agriculture contributed only 7 percent. By comparison, the West Bank and the Gaza Strip were labor-surplus economies with little industrial development and low levels of investment. In 1969 agriculture in the territories still accounted for 37 percent of total domestic product while industry and construction accounted only for 13 percent.

The 1967 war suddenly brought into close proximity these different economies that had been separated for nearly two decades. While no exact historical analogy fits this situation, there are numerous examples of intimate economic relationships developing between high income, capital-intensive regions and low income, labor-surplus areas. Examples would include the historical relationships between Ireland and the United Kingdom, between the West Indies and the United Kingdom, between Southern Italy and other parts of Europe, between parts of North Africa and the French economy, or between Puerto Rico and the United States. The economic relationship between Israel and the West Bank and the Gaza Strip shares some characteristics with economic linkages developed between rich and poor regions observable in many parts of the world—though the political circumstances are unique. Even in strictly economic terms there are a number of special characteristics of the Israel-West Bank-Gaza Strip relationship, so the comparisons must be handled with care. Four distinguishing features of the situation are important.

The first is the simple geographical fact of short distances between centers of population. It has permitted daily or weekly commuting—the latter is illegal but widespread—into Israel by West Bank and Gaza Strip Palestinians. Their employment in Israel has not involved actual migration—migration that, in any event, is prohibited by Israel. The short distances have also meant that Israeli industry can sell as readily in the West Bank and Gaza Strip as in Israel itself.[2]

A second striking characteristic is that the new pattern of economic interpenetration evolved very swiftly. The picture that emerges in the following chapters indicates that during the period of Israeli rule the economic situation in the West Bank and the Gaza Strip has shifted dramatically. Having started from a point of total economic isolation from Israel, the two territories now are at a point where their connection with Israel has become the predominant external economic contact. Because this transition was so abrupt, some of its more subtle and long-term consequences have not yet had time to work themselves out. It is likely, for example, that the high growth rates achieved thus far cannot be sustained through the same economic mechanisms—because these rates reflected the economic dynamics of the transition rather than performance sustainable over a longer period.

A third distinguishing characteristic is that Israel has exercised exclusive and complete control over the West Bank and Gaza Strip economies. In this sense the balance of authority in the formulation of economic policy is similar to that exercised by a metropolitan power over a non-self-governing territory: West Bank and Gaza Strip Palestinians have not participated in the political process that has set the major economic policies affecting them or that has supervised the overall implementation of these policies.

Finally, political and security factors have played some role in shaping Israel's economic policies toward the territories. Trade across the Jordan is limited, in part, because of Israel's wish to control all transactions over the bridges for military and security reasons. The reluctance of Israeli businessmen to establish a presence in the Arab towns of the territories derives, in part, from uncertainty over their political future. And the absence of large-scale public investment by the Israeli government in either the West Bank or the Gaza Strip rests, in part, on a desire to avoid an impression of "economic annexation," to avoid a situation in which the territories are a significant net tax burden on the citizens of Israel, and to avoid having to force a decision on the whole question of the political future of the territories—a deeply divisive question in Israeli politics.

Rather than pretend to assess fully the detailed consequences of the post-1967 situation on the internal economic life of the West Bank, the Gaza Strip, Israel, and Jordan, this study describes and interprets the major characteristics of the economic interconnections that have emerged among these four economies since 1967. The following chapters are organized to clarify the main trends of recent years and to provide an understanding of the broad economic setting for future developments. The analytic framework of this study can help answer the questions "What has happened?" and "What light does this throw on the nature of future economic options in the region?" But no simple and definitive answer can be offered to the questions "Has the impact been economically desirable?" and "Will the set of relationships lead to the economic development of the West Bank and the Gaza Strip?" To see why answers to these questions are so elusive, at least within this study's terms of reference, it is useful to look briefly at views about the effects of economic exchanges between highly-developed and less-developed regions elsewhere. These views provide some insight into the nature of the economic process examined here, and they facilitate informed judgment where the data are inadequate. But they also suggest why the consequences of such interrelationships cannot be evaluated in neutral technocratic terms acceptable even to most professional economists. For among economists, the consequences, in terms of the well-being of poor regions, that flow from economic interaction with richer regions have as often been matters of controversy as of agreement.

The history of colonial independence and of regional separatist movements is rich in debate about the economic and social consequences of such dependent economic relationships. And in this larger perspective the economic connection developed between Israel and the West Bank and the Gaza Strip is of a kind that would be in any circumstances a source of serious controversy—quite apart from the controversy inherent in a situation so inextricably tied to the entire Arab-Israeli conflict. The problem is, of course, that economic "facts" are themselves often a matter of selection, perception, and interpretation.

The international movement of labor often creates social tension. The employment of large numbers of manual laborers from another society, resulting in concentration of minority groups in unskilled labor occupations, often politically disenfranchised, has very typically been a source of controversy. It emanates from both communities involved in the transaction, despite the apparent "economic rationality" of the process. A migrant or commuting laborer into an industrial economy may enjoy an income that on the one hand is superior to his previous income but that on the other hand places him at the bottom of the economic scale in the host economy. Depending on which frame of reference is used, he is either enjoying the benefits of a high income, or he is underprivileged. He begins to see himself as exploited—vulnerable, and relegated to the bottom of the economic ladder—while workers who are citizens in the host economy sometimes perceive a threat from the potential competition of "cheap" labor.

Trading patterns that tend to concentrate the more sophisticated industrial processes in more highly developed regions are equally a matter of controversy. In most developing countries, no matter what benefits might be gained from periods of growth through specialization in primary commodity production, this form of specialization is widely seen as leaving the primary producing region in a vulnerable neo-colonial position vis-à-vis the industrial powers. What is seen by one set of economists as a mutually beneficial system of economic exchange is seen by another group as an essentially unequal, exploitative relationship. As economies with different levels of development are brought into closer economic contact, expectations change and new comparisons are made. The terms at which the sets of exchanges are struck become contentious. Questions about whether prices or wages are fair to this or that group or region are, after all, the normal fare of debates between spokesmen for the Third World countries and the West. While one interpretation can envisage the expansion of private capital movements and the growth of existing trade as the key to the solution of the problem of underdevelopment, another sees that pattern of neo-colonial relationships as the essence of the *problem* rather than the core of the solution.

Whatever the merits of the economic arguments offered by both sides in such debates, it is a chastening thought that the development of economic exchanges between poor and rich regions elsewhere in the world have resulted in such widely divergent fundamental interpretations. In view of the persistence of these divergent interpretations on a worldwide scale, it should not be surprising that they appear frequently in contending arguments about the pattern of economic relations that now links Israel to the two less developed territories. For here too the interpretations stem not just from particular conflicts of real interest, but also from more general differences in economic and social analysis. There are indeed two quite different paradigms in use. And as the prologue to this study indicated, both paradigms have influenced evaluations of the West Bank-Gaza Strip situation, as well as discussions of the role Israel traditionally has hoped to play economically in the Middle East.

Economic developments in the two territories have tended to bring these contending paradigms into sharp focus. Once the appropriate environment was established by Israeli public policy, the market dynamics lent to the resulting economic process an apparent naturalness and logic that can readily appeal to traditional, neo-classical economists. Many economic agents responded to market opportunities offered by the differences in the availability of resources between Israel and the West Bank and the Gaza Strip—labor, capital, skills, natural endowment, and so on. Because of the size of wage differentials, particularly powerful forces operated through the labor market. The resulting exchanges conform to expectations derived from trade theory, and the high growth achieved in the territories would seem to justify the conclusion that the exchanges have brought mutual benefits to the participants. However, the principles involved are not straightforward—as they were not, for example, in the British debate in the early seventies over membership in the European Economic Community. The economic consequences of such interregional or international economic relationships, including those that have emerged since 1967 between Israel and the West Bank and Gaza Strip economies, need to be assessed in light of a number of general economic propositions.

A common market or customs union arrangement diverts trade, building up exchanges within the arrangement at the expense of possible development or relationships with areas outside. Expensive goods produced within the market may have to be purchased, rather than goods at cheaper world market prices. Representatives of less advanced regions have often argued that benefits within common markets flow disproportionately to the most industrially advanced member, in the absence of powerful corrective policies.

Industry, largely dependent on the internal market, depends upon protection and enjoys the economies of scale reaped from the enlarged market. Industrial development for the less advanced region is limited by competition from the more industrially advanced member. Particularly where the total market is small, industry will tend to gravitate to existing centers of industrial activities. Even if participation in such an arrangement is to be the net benefit of a region, typically the benefits will not be reaped by those who bear the costs. Whatever the overall or "average" interest, particular groups will emerge who reap a greater advantage or suffer a greater loss than is typical, and they may align themselves for or against integration accordingly.

Economic consequences can also be profound, if sometimes quite subtle, in the long term for the structure of the economy and the societies involved. Thus, trade may reinforce the initial conditions that created the tendency to specialize, which may have long-term disadvantages. The literature on underdevelopment includes, for example, extensive debates regarding the dangers of specialization in a narrow range of primary commodity production. Specializing in the supply of manual labor perhaps has even greater dangers. To quote Albert Hirschman:

> The opponents of free trade have often pointed out that for a variety of reasons it is imprudent and harmful for a country to become specialized along certain product lines in accordance with the dictates of comparative advantage. Whatever the merit of these critical arguments, they would certainly acquire over-whelming weight if the question arose whether a country should allow itself to become specialized not just along certain commodity lines, but along factor-of-production lines. Very few countries would ever consciously wish to specialize in unskilled labor, while foreigners with comparative advantage in entrepreneurship, management, skilled labor, and capital took over these functions, replacing inferior "local talent."[3]

In the most general terms, market relationships are often not between equals. Often an asymmetry is clearest when a monopolist faces a large number of customers and is able to sway the balance of advantage in an exchange in his favor. The advantage in a trading relationship will usually be biased strongly on one side of the bargain or the other, and uncontrolled market transactions will therefore be particularly advantageous to one side.

These general economic propositions take on particular weight in the context of the West Bank and Gaza Strip. These are largely agricultural economies, made up of small economic units and an unorganized labor force with a low level of technological development, linked to a highly organized economy with a heavily protected industrial sector and a sophisticated level of technology. It is true that powerful expansionary effects can typically benefit the poorer economy. In the short term, employment opportunities widen, incomes rise, and growth rates accelerate as a result of contact with advanced economy—even granting the possibility that such performance can be temporary rather than permanent. And in the long term, access to more advanced technology may have a positive impact on productivity. But the poor economy also finds itself operating as a captive market for the industrial products of the more developed one. Its agricultural products receive little protection or subsidization; its workers are the most vulnerable group in an otherwise highly organized labor market; and what investment opportunities emerge for the investors of the poorer economy are largely in a limited range of activities that play a complementary role to the more experienced and better-organized businesses of the richer economy.

In this particular context, moreover, the poorer economies—lacking sovereignty, of course—have had no opportunity to use traditional policy instruments such as tariffs or exchange rate adjustments to serve their own economic objectives. Unable to modify public policy decisions or the market process in order to meet local needs, the West Bank and the Gaza Strip economies have been affected by Israeli tariffs, exchange rate adjustments, and fiscal and monetary policy—necessarily framed to meet the needs of the Israeli economy. The territories have had to be the passive recipients of the effects of developments in an Israeli economy subject to considerable inflationary pressures and associated currency devaluations.

A basic element in the economic perspective that this study adopts toward the period of Israeli rule over the territories is an attitude about criteria for testing what has happened economically since 1967. In general, the implications of any economic arrangements, past or future, cannot be tested in the abstract but only against some alternative, foregone opportunity. In economic discussion that alternative is often left implicit; nevertheless it is not satisfactory to assume that it is simply the *status quo ante*. Developments in the period after 1967 should not be judged solely by comparison to the situation existing before the 1967 war. Nor can we fall back on the economist's old device of *ceteris paribus:* we cannot examine only one feature of the economic picture on the assumption that the larger economic environment can be treated as given and that the costs can be measured against specified alternative possible uses of the resources involved. In this case, the policies being evaluated affect the total economic picture. And extremely complicated assumptions would be required to test actual developments against conceivable alternatives. An overall verdict on the economic developments during the period 1967-75 for the

West Bank and the Gaza Strip is especially problematic because the criteria used must depend upon the alternative political scenarios judged to have been either probable or desirable and upon the economic implications attributed to them. However, to make these comparisons would involve an exercise in considerable analytic arbitrariness and no little fantasy. And, of course, the utility of such a speculative exercise for all protagonists is unclear in the present circumstances because preferences for particular future political options have little to do with the likely economic benefits expected.

A final cautionary point concerns the impact of economic growth on social and political stability in the West Bank and the Gaza Strip. The notion that economic growth and the expansion of income and job opportunities reduces social tension and the underlying basis for political conflict in some straightforward fashion is as simplistic and untenable in this as in other politically-charged situations. Political awareness and mobilization, as well as crystallization of nationalist aspirations, are as likely to follow periods of economic expansion and changing levels of expectation and confidence as periods of stagnation. In short, no simple political conclusions flow from an analysis of economic developments in the territories since 1967. And no credible political conclusions about the future can rest solely on judgments—however well considered in technical economic terms—of an essentially economic character.

In the spirit of these conceptual observations and caveats, the framework used here to order the multiple relationships now linking Israel, the West Bank, the Gaza Strip and Jordan identifies three interconnections of paramount importance, each described more fully in subsequent chapters as far as the incomplete data will allow. These are the interconnections operating through (a) the labor market, (b) trade in commodities, and (c) financial flows and linkages. On each of these dimensions, the broad trends can be summarized briefly.

THE LABOR MARKET

The labor market heads this list both because the movement of labor has been the most dramatic economic factor in the entire picture since 1967 and because of its great potential social significance.

During the years 1968-73, the Israeli economy enjoyed a period of sustained growth, resulting after 1969 in a tight labor market. After an initial brief period in which Israeli unemployment levels were high enough to discourage policies that would allow commuting laborers from the territories to compete for scarce jobs, the Israeli employment picture changed, and cheap labor from the West Bank and from the Gaza Strip was drawn increasingly into employment in Israel. The process moved semi-employed peasants and unemployed laborers from the territories into the Israeli economy at the lower end of the economic scale as members of the manual working class; at the same time, members of the middle economic strata of West Bank and Gaza Strip society found themselves with a narrower range of economic opportunities and a consequent need to find new economic roles in relation to the Israeli-dominated pattern of economic development in the territories. For the better-educated Palestinians, the absence of full-scale governmental functions limits somewhat the employment opportunities that might otherwise be available, although the existing Israeli-administered bureaucracy in the territories, as well as the UNRWA bureaucracies, is staffed almost totally by Palestinian personnel. The available data on the two economies indicate overwhelmingly that wage income earned in Israel was the major source of their economic growth in the period 1969-73. Palestinians from the territories, mainly those who were more highly skilled and educated, also moved in substantial numbers both before and after 1967 to jobs in other parts of the Middle East, Europe, and North and South America.[4]

Several economic and social implications of these labor market connections are contentious. As already suggested, West Bank and Gaza Strip Palestinians working in Israel have enjoyed an increase in income, often substantial, over what could be earned in the territories. For these workers, concentrated in the least privileged segment of the Israeli labor market, the passage of time could very well accentuate the negative aspects of specializing in the role of the poor working class in Israeli society and could weigh ever more heavily against the immediate economic advantages of increased income. Second, the massive withdrawal of labor from the territories themselves threatens to create problems for the local economy, for example, by leaving local enterprises faced with labor scarcity and pressure on the local wage level. The extreme long-term prospect would be for the local economies to be reduced to the role of a dormitory for manual labor and for an intensification of an emerging bias in the structure and skills of the Palestinian labor force. Third, the economic burden falls heavily on those members of the population faced with increased prices—stimulated partly by increased labor costs—but who for one reason or another do not enjoy improved employment opportunities. Many of the better educated fall into this category. And, finally, the cyclical vulnerability of Palestinian laborers from the territories to job loss in the event of a general downturn in the Israeli economy is a prospect that was quite clearly evident as the Israeli economy moved deeper into recession in 1975. Indeed, given the highly concentrated sectoral and occupational structure of the commuting workers, as well as their organizational weakness, the local impact of any recession in Israel is likely to be magnified—and for some residents, at least, perceived as even more serious because of rises in local prices as a result of Israel's inflation.

THE COMMODITY MARKET

The external connections of the West Bank and the Gaza Strip through commodity trade exhibit a pattern characteristic of less-developed regions. The territories are primarily producers of agricultural goods and importers of manufactures. With the creation of protected trading links with Israel and the severe limitation (in the case of Jordan) or elimination (in the case of Egypt) of the previous import channels, the main source of imports became the Israeli economy. Some of these imports, in turn, are Israeli imports from the rest of the world, either incorporated into Israeli products or trans-shipped to the territories in their imported form.

The West Bank-Gaza Strip export trade to the East Bank and the rest of the world has continued since 1967. But an increasing share of exports went to the Israeli economy, either to be consumed in Israel or to become part of the Israeli export trade. Israel rapidly became both the dominant trading partner for the territories and also the trading intermediary between them and the world market. The West Bank and the Gaza Strip have provided an expanded, protected market for Israeli products, and, by virtue of the Israeli tariff barriers, consumers in the two territories find their access to overseas commodities limited.

It would be difficult to make the claim that West Bank and Gaza Strip economies gain advantages from being linked to the Israeli economy through trade connections. Because of the high levels of Israeli tariffs, West Bank and Gaza Strip consumers either have to pay high prices for imports from overseas or to purchase them from a high-cost Israeli supplier. Yet the high levels of protection are of little use to West Bank and Gaza Strip producers; typically they are not in a good position to compete with Israeli sources of supply.

The trade benefits resulting from the connection are mainly reaped by Israel. Some Arab businesses have benefited from co-operating with Israeli firms in the subcontracting business, and some have been able to market specialized products to Arab consumers in Israel. Consumers in general have also benefited from access to subsidized Israeli agricultural products, although this is likely to be at the expense of local agriculture; moreover, as Israeli subsidies have been lifted recently on certain items to force belt-tightening on citizens of Israel, the benefits to residents of the territories have diminished.

The development of manufacturing industry in the West Bank and Gaza Strip has remained very limited. Given the competition from Israeli products, the rising costs of labor, and the absence of any specific policies to encourage industry, there is little reason to expect any change in this sector. In a subsequent chapter, the implicit costs of this absence of industrial growth are assessed: Does it represent the stunting of potential growth? Does it reinforce structural imbalance in the economy? Or is the potential for West Bank and Gaza Strip industrial development exaggerated by critics of Israeli policy?

The additional, and possibly the most serious, long-term cost of the trade pattern to West Bank and Gaza Strip business is the loss of opportunity to develop markets outside Israel. While the open bridges policy has maintained a flow of trade across the River Jordan, this has been of diminishing relative importance to the local economies. The exact extent of foreign trading opportunities foregone, it must be admitted, is a matter of conjecture. The long-term development of trade with the Middle East would itself depend on the local pattern of investment and industrial and commercial development.

FINANCIAL LINKS

The financial linkages are more difficult to observe. British and Arab commercial banks operating in the territories before 1967 were closed just after Israeli rule was established, and they were never successfully replaced by Israeli banks. Despite the degree of interconnection between the West Bank and the Gaza Strip and the Israeli economy through the labor market and through trade, the territories have retained a substantial degree of financial autonomy. They have done this through continuing private financial links with Jordan and other parts of the Middle East, continuing monetary links with Jordan through the circulation of the dinar in the West Bank, and some continuing fiscal connections between the Jordanian government and the West Bank. Although trade and labor has moved between the territories and Israel, there has been nothing like a similar movement in capital in either direction. Israeli public and private investment in economic development programs for the territories remained minor—for reasons indicated earlier. And the West Bank-Gaza Strip Palestinians have utilized the Israeli banking system only to a very limited degree.

An unusual monetary situation has developed within the West Bank whereby the Jordanian dinar has continued to circulate, alongside the Israeli pound, as legal tender. The West Bank therefore participates in two different monetary systems, that of Israel and that of Jordan. However, this is one area in which it is particularly difficult to establish with any precision what is happening. While rough estimates are available for the amount of Jordanian currency circulating in the West Bank, there is little information about the form in which the residents of the West Bank and the Gaza Strip hold their accumulated assets.

In addition to evaluating the impact of the links which have developed, it is also important to take account of important absences of connections, which in other circumstances might have been expected. The lack of the movement of Israeli private capital into the territories, which was noted above, represents an important limitation on the degree of economic integration between Israel and the territories. Connections between Israeli industry and the territories has been through the movement of labor or through sub-contracting rather than through the creation of new Israeli-owned plants in the territories. This has meant that the external impact on the internal economic structure of the West Bank and the Gaza Strip has been less than if there had been exposure to Israeli, or other, foreign investment.

Taking the labor, commodity, and financial interconnections together, it is clear that a varied and often dense network of economic links has grown since 1967 among the economies of the West Bank, the Gaza Strip, Israel, and Jordan. The detailed story of these interactions is complex, and the economic life of the area has been pervasively affected. A more extensive look at this story will make it evident that it is relatively straightforward to describe how this network of linkages has developed and to analyze its likely evolution. It will be equally evident that evaluation of the merits and demerits of these economic processes is very far from straightforward, both in practice and in principle.

Footnotes

1. An excellent study of the immediate post-1967 factors at work within Israeli politics and their effect on early economic decisions is Ann Mosely Lesch, *Israel's Occupation of the West Bank: The First Two Years* (Santa Monica, California: The Rand Corporation, 1970), pp. 21-36.

2. For example, the distance from Nablus to Tel Aviv is only thirty-five miles. Hebron is about fifty-five miles from Tel Aviv, and Gaza forty-five miles. Distances between Jerusalem and the main West Bank centers of Nablus and Hebron are even less, thirty and twenty miles respectively.

3. *How to Divest in Latin America and Why,* Essays in International Finance No. 76 (Princeton, New Jersey: Princeton University Department of Economics, 1969), p. 5.

4. For more detail see Nabeel Shaath, "High Level Palestinian Manpower," *Journal of Palestine Studies* 1 (1971-72): 80-95; and Lafi Jaafari, "The Brain Drain to the United States: The Migration of Jordanian and Palestinian Professionals and Students," *Journal of Palestine Studies* 3 (1973-74): 119-131.

Chapter 3

The Labor Market

THE LABOR FORCE

In September, 1967, the West Bank (excluding East Jerusalem) and the Gaza Strip had a total population of 986,000—596,000 of whom were in the West Bank, and 390,000 of whom were in the Gaza Strip and the adjacent area of the North Sinai coast west to El-Arish. In addition, the 65,000 Palestinians of East Jerusalem had been incorporated by Israel by the annexation, although they had retained their Jordanian citizenship. During the summer of 1967, a large number of Palestinians from the territories, particularly the West Bank, crossed the River Jordan to take up residence on the East Bank—over 200,000 people were involved in this movement.

Until the beginning of 1969, the population of the two territories continued to decline as a result of emigration, falling to a low of 942,000 at the end of 1968—584,000 in the West Bank, and 358,000 in Gaza. From then on, however, a high rate of natural increase in population and a decline of net emigration restored a high population growth.

By 1973 the combined population of the West Bank and Gaza was 1,051,000—of whom 522,000 were of working age. The rather low figure of 197,700 were active members of the labor force. The population growth rate for the two territories had risen

Table III-1

Sources of Population Increase
(In Thousands)

Year	Population at beginning of year	Population at end of year	Natural increase	Yearly rate of increase
The West Bank				
1967 Census	595.9	585.5	3.0	−1.7
1968	585.5	584.1	14.1	−0.2
1969	584.1	599.7	14.4	+2.7
1970	599.7	610.3	15.6	+1.8
1971	610.3	625.6	17.8	+2.5
1972	625.6	639.3	18.8	+2.2
1973	639.3	657.4	17.8	+2.8
The Gaza Strip and North Sinai				
1967 Census	389.7	379.9	3.3	−2.5
1968	379.9	357.8	9.2	−5.8
1969	357.8	365.5	10.6	+2.2
1970	365.5	372.4	10.2	+1.9
1971	372.4	381.8	11.8	+2.5
1972	381.8	390.7	12.7	+2.3
1973	390.7	405.4	13.0	+3.4

SOURCE: *Statistical Abstract of Israel 1974*
(Jerusalem: Central Bureau of Statistics,
1974), Table xxvi/1, p. 682.

to 3.2 percent per annum. (See Table III-1 for population growth rate data, 1967-73.) By comparison, the total population of Israel, including East Jerusalem, had reached 3,307,500 by the end of 1973—2,810,000 Jewish and 497,100 Arab and other minorities. The growth rate of the Jewish population was 3.2 percent, but about half of this was made up of net immigration; the growth rate of the rest of the population was 4.3 percent, based on the extraordinarily high estimated rate of natural increase of 4 percent per annum.

In the population of the West Bank and the Gaza Strip, there is a relative preponderance of women in the age group ranging from 25-50 years old. (See Tables III-2 and III-3 for detailed breakdown.) This reflects two facts: among younger groups males show a greater tendency to seek education outside the area and, most important, at all age levels males from the Gaza Strip and

Table III-2

Population by Sex and Age, December 31, 1973
(In Thousands)

Age	The West Bank			The Gaza Strip and North Sinai			Total		
	Females	Males	Total	Females	Males	Total	Females	Males	Total
Total	327.4	330.0	657.4	205.3	200.0	405.3	532.7	530.0	1,062.7
0-4	55.6	63.0	118.6	35.3	39.6	74.9	90.9	102.5	193.4
5-9	47.2	53.1	100.3	29.9	32.9	62.8	77.1	86.0	163.1
10-14	48.0	52.9	100.9	28.7	31.1	59.8	76.7	84.0	160.7
15-19	36.2	40.3	76.5	23.9	25.8	49.7	60.1	66.1	126.2
20-24	24.2	24.2	48.4	18.0	17.0	35.0	42.2	41.2	83.5
25-29	18.9	15.1	34.0	13.7	9.1	22.8	32.6	24.2	56.8
30-34	16.9	12.0	28.9	10.9	6.1	17.0	27.9	18.1	45.9
35-39	15.4	11.2	26.6	9.9	6.7	16.6	25.3	17.8	43.1
40-44	15.0	11.2	26.2	9.7	7.2	16.9	24.7	18.3	43.1
45-49	12.6	10.1	22.7	7.5	6.4	13.9	20.1	16.5	36.6
50-54	8.8	7.9	16.9	4.9	4.9	9.8	13.9	12.9	26.8
55-59	6.8	6.3	13.2	3.6	3.3	6.9	10.4	9.7	20.1
60-64	6.1	6.1	12.2	2.8	2.7	5.5	8.9	8.8	17.6
65-69	6.0	6.1	12.0	2.5	2.7	5.2	8.5	8.8	17.3
70-74	3.4	4.7	8.1	1.2	2.1	3.3	4.6	6.9	11.5
75+	6.0	5.8	11.8	2.7	2.5	5.2	8.8	8.2	17.0

SOURCE: *Statistical Abstract of Israel 1974*, Table xxvi/3, p. 683.

Table III-3

Population by Age, Showing Also the Ratio of Males to Females Per 1,000 Females

(In Thousands)

Year	Total	Ages 0-14	Ages 15-29	Ages 30-44	Ages 45-64	Ages 65 +	Males per 1,000 females
The West Bank							
1967 Census	595.9*	286.6	119.7	82.7	64.6	39.1	985
1968	584.1	285.8	121.8	79.4	61.5	35.6	990
1969	599.7	292.4	131.0	80.8	62.0	33.5	997
1970	610.3	296.4	137.3	82.3	62.5	31.8	1,000
1971	625.6	305.0	145.4	83.0	62.4	29.8	1,005
1972	639.3	311.7	147.7	80.0	65.4	34.5	1,001
1973	657.4	319.7	159.0	81.7	64.9	32.0	1,008
The Gaza Strip and North Sinai							
1967 Census	389.7*	194.6	83.2	55.6	34.9	18.3	943
1968	357.8	179.3	81.6	49.6	31.4	15.9	942
1969	365.5	182.3	87.3	49.7	31.6	14.6	949
1970	372.4	185.1	91.8	50.4	31.5	13.6	953
1971	381.8	189.0	97.9	50.8	31.5	12.6	954
1972	390.7	191.4	99.0	49.4	35.9	15.0	962
1973	405.4	197.5	107.5	50.4	36.2	13.8	974

SOURCE: *Statistical Abstract of Israel 1974*, Table xxvi/2, p. 682.

* Includes age not known.

the West Bank seek employment in other parts of the Middle East and beyond.

The importance of such migration is indicated by the data in Table III-4, derived from the Israeli census of the territories conducted in September, 1967. In that year about one-third of the households in the West Bank, and almost one-quarter in the Gaza Strip, had sons or daughters staying outside the territories. In absolute numbers, 77,000 from the West Bank and 28,000 from Gaza were living away from their parental homes. If one takes account of less immediate family connections, the numbers leaving either for work or study but retaining family links must be significantly greater.

The essential characteristics of the Palestinian labor force remaining in the West Bank and the Gaza Strip in 1967 can be briefly summarized:

Education: The adult male population had enjoyed considerable access to schooling, particularly by comparison with less developed countries at similar levels of income. For the younger age groups, some schooling was virtually universal for males. In the 15-19 year age groups, more than 95 percent had experienced some schooling in both the West Bank and the Gaza Strip; in the West Bank, almost one-half of that age group had experienced nine years or more, while in the Gaza Strip, that figure almost reached two-thirds. For the older groups, the figures are much lower. Nevertheless, for the entire adult male population (15 years plus), nearly half had enjoyed five years or more education, 47 percent on the West Bank, and 49 percent in the Gaza Strip; those having experienced eleven years or more amounted to 10 percent in the West Bank, and 17 percent in the Gaza Strip. Interestingly, educational levels were somewhat higher in the Gaza Strip than in the West Bank, and also in the Gaza Strip they were slightly higher among refugees than non-refugees—some indication of UNRWA's contribution. Among the older groups, it may be supposed that these figures are probably biased downwards in describing the education level of the total Palestinian population since those away from home would have above-average education. The figures on women's education indicate a trend towards raising earlier low levels of female participation, with a sizable majority of the youngest age group having experienced some schooling.

Employment: Levels of employment before the 1967 war had been low. A high proportion of those who fled in 1967 came from

Table III-4

Households With Sons or Daughters Outside the Territories in 1967*

	The West Bank	The Gaza Strip and North Sinai
Total number of households	119,148	66,817
Percent of households with sons or daughters staying outside Israeli occupied territories	33.1	24.0
Absolute numbers of sons or daughters staying outside Israeli occupied territories	77,468	27,697
Percent of sons or daughters who reside in:		
Jordan (East Bank)	40.8	6.6
Kuwait	33.5	9.5
Saudi Arabia	5.8	15.6
Lebanon	2.1	2.8
Iraq and Syria	2.2	1.4
Egypt	2.9	55.5
Europe, America and Oceania	11.1	1.9
Other countries in Asia and Africa	1.6	6.7

* All figures are estimates based on a sample survey and subject to error.

SOURCE: Israel Defence Forces, *Demographic Characteristics of the Population in the Administered Areas,* Publication No. 3 of the Census of Population 1967 (Jerusalem: Central Bureau of Statistics, 1968), pp. 30-32, 62-64.

refugee camps, and almost certainly included a higher proportion of unemployed than would be typical of the entire population. Nevertheless, of the adult male population remaining in the West Bank after the 1967 war, only about 60 percent had been employed prior to the war, while in the Gaza Strip the figure was 55 percent. (See Table III-5.) Employment among the best educated (nine or more years of schooling) was lower than among the less well educated, but it is also true that the best educated were in the youngest age group (15-24 years). Women have had only a minimal role in the employed work force as statistically recorded, their major economic role being within the family unit, including providing labor for the family farm.

Table III-5

Work Participation Among Males Employed Before the 1967 War, by Age

	15-24	25-34	35-44	45-54	55-64	65+	Total
The West Bank							
Total Number	40,488	23,707	21,999	15,740	15,591	20,474	137,999
employed	16,700	20,630	19,046	12,581	9,505	6,057	84,519
Percent employed	41.2	87.0	86.6	79.9	61.0	29.6	61.2
The Gaza Strip and North Sinai							
Total Number	26,568	14,115	14,461	8,958	7,426	9,365	80,893
employed	7,884	12,231	12,298	6,858	4,042	2,160	45,473
Percent employed	29.7	86.7	85.0	76.6	54.4	23.1	56.2

SOURCE: Israel Defence Forces, *Labour Force, Part I,*
Publication No. 4 of the Census of
Population 1967 (Jerusalem: Central
Bureau of Statistics, 1968), Table A, p. vii
and Table H, p. xiv.

The Structure of Employment: As shown in Table III-6, the West Bank work force on the eve of the 1967 war was divided roughly equally between agriculture, 34.2 percent; construction, industry and crafts, mining and quarrying, 33.5 percent; and the service sectors (including transport, public service, trade and professions), 32.3 percent. In the Gaza Strip the relative importance of agricultural and related occupations was much lower, being only 22 percent. Thus an increasingly well-educated population produced a relatively small employed work force. Even before the 1967 war unemployment levels were high, and the immediate impact of postwar economic dislocation pushed them even higher. The active work force was small relative to the total population, because of the youthful structure of the population, the number of adult male absences, and the low participation of women in paid employment.

EMPLOYMENT IN THE ISRAELI ECONOMY

In the first year of occupation, Palestinian laborers were not allowed to seek work in Israel because authorities feared that such employment would aggravate unemployment problems in Israel.

Table III-6

Percent, by Economic Branch, of Employed Men in Israel, the West Bank and the Gaza Strip*

	Israeli Arabs** (1966 Labour Force survey)	West Bank (1967 survey)	Gaza Strip (1967 survey)
Agriculture, forestry, and fishing	36.3	34.6	23.9
Mines, industry, and crafts	16.3	15.1	13.9
Construction and public works	22.1	15.6	9.2
Electricity, water, and sanitary services	0.9	0.9	1.3
Commerce, banking and insurance	7.4	12.3	16.3
Transport, freight, storage, and communications	6.7	6.8	8.5
Services	10.3	14.7	26.9
Total	100.0	100.0	100.0

*Figures on the West Bank and the Gaza Strip are based on a sample survey rather than a complete census and, therefore, are subject to sampling errors.

**Also includes non-Arabs and non-Jews, who comprise less than 5 percent of the total Israeli populations.

SOURCE: Israel Defence Forces, *Labour Force, Part I.* Table M, p. xxi.

By July, 1968, however, a labor shortage emerged in Israel, and West Bank and Gaza Strip residents were permitted to seek work in Israel, and met an Israeli need for unskilled day laborers.

After 1969, employment in Israel of Palestinians from the territories increased sharply. From some 12,000 in 1968 and 1969, the number rose to 68,000 by the third quarter of 1973; and, after a decline as a result of the 1973 war, it rose again to reach a peak of 78,800 in the third quarter of 1974. It has subsequently declined as the Israeli economy moved into recession. The actual numbers have been significantly higher than those totals at any given time, however, because some workers commute illegally and have never been reflected in the official estimates.[1]

By mid-1974 employment in Israel accounted for 31.7 percent of total employment of West Bank and Gaza Strip residents. The quantitative importance of employment in Israel as a form of *wage labor* is even greater, since a high proportion of employment in the territories, particularly in the West Bank, is self-employment in agriculture, crafts, and the service sector. Thus, 1973 figures show that 59,300 of the total of 119,000 employees *(i.e.,* wage laborers) from the West Bank and the Gaza Strip were employees in Israel, that is 49.8 percent, or one-half.

As Table III-7 indicates, throughout this period roughly half the jobs in Israel were generated in the construction industry, which enjoyed a period of considerable boom. Between 1968 and 1972 Israeli expenditure on construction more than doubled in real terms, rising from 2,048,000 to 4,347,500 Israeli pounds at constant 1970 prices. By 1973, 30,000 West Bank and Gaza Strip Palestinians worked in that industry.

The relative importance of West Bank and Gaza Strip labor in the total Israeli work force has not been great. Even at its peak, it accounted for less than 6 percent of total employment, and 7 percent of total employees. However, the concentration of West Bank and Gaza Strip labor in the construction sector has been very significant—by 1973 one-quarter of the work force and an even higher proportion of employees (some 28 percent). Just over one-half of the employees of the construction industry are recruited from the two territories and from the non-Jewish population of Israel (including East Jerusalem), and during the industry's rapid growth between 1970-73, three-fifths (59 percent) of the increase in employees came from the two territories. Overall, it can be roughly estimated that some 12 percent of those involved in manual labor in the Israeli economy in 1973 were West Bank and Gaza Strip residents.[2]

These indicators all suggest that Palestinian labor from the West Bank and the Gaza Strip played a significant role in the expansion of the Israeli economy during the period 1968-73. The numbers are not so large that withdrawal of this labor could be expected to cause economic collapse. But for the particular sectors that have become highly dependent on this manpower, its absence would imply difficulties and the need for a considerable reallocation of the Israeli work force. At any rate, there is no doubt the

Table III-7

Percent, by Economic Sector and Place of Work, of Employed Persons from the West Bank, the Gaza Strip and North Sinai

	1968	1969	1970	1971	1972	1973
In Israel						
Agriculture	20	17	24.4	22.3	23.1	19.3
Industry	20	17	11.6	14.8	17.1	18.1
Construction	40	42	54.3	52.3	49.5	51.7
Other	20	24	9.7	10.6	10.3	10.9
Total number	5,000	12,000	20,600	33,800	52,400	61,300
In the Territories						
Agriculture	35	42	38.7	36.8	33.5	31.3
Industry	14	13	13.8	13.8	13.9	15.1
Construction	10	9	8.4	5.6	6.2	6.4
Other	41	36	39.1	43.8	46.4	47.2
Total number	130,000	151,000	152,700	142,700	136,300	133,400

SOURCES: *Statistical Abstract of Israel 1974*, p. 705
and Arie Bregman, *Economic Growth in the
Administered Areas, 1968-1973*
(Jerusalem: Bank of Israel Research
Department, 1975), p. 32.

growth of the Israeli economy was appreciably higher between 1967 and 1973 because of the ready availability of this labor.

Because the expansion of Palestinian employment in the Israeli economy took place during an upswing in the Israeli economy, the question arises whether there is likely to be cyclical change as that economy moves into recession. With heavy concentration in the construction industry and the more manual occupations, and with no organizational basis for bargaining, laborers from the territories would seem to be highly vulnerable, their unemployment levels probably magnifying Israeli economic fluctuations.

When Israel moved into recession in 1975, employment of the territories' residents turned down in the second quarter. According to preliminary and incomplete data available at this writing, the employment of workers from the West Bank and the Gaza Strip had fallen back by the third quarter of the year by 11 percent from the peak of one year before (70,000 compared to 79,000), and was continuing to fall.[3]

Part of the slack was taken up by an increase in employment of 4,000 in the territories, probably one result of the revival in construction activity in 1974 and 1975.[4] A shift in employment back to the local economies may, in fact, be seen as a desirable consequence of the Israeli recession. However, it is also the case that there has been an increase in those workers who have to cross the Jordan River to seek work. This may be interpreted as a result both of the slackening in the Israeli job market and of the labor-scarcity that has developed in Jordan as a consequence of economic expansion.

The pattern of Palestinian labor participation in Israel's economy is quite typical of other situations where there has been attraction of labor from rural to urban areas, and from backward regions to urban centers. In this instance, the commuting phenomenon has been facilitated by Israeli training programs conducted in the territories, concentrating on such basic building skills as bricklaying, tiling, and electrical fitting. This started as a program of intensive short courses and is now geared more to training high school graduates in longer courses—practical in nature, aimed at developing specific, but limited skills. Critics argue that this training program merely perpetuates the bias that confines Palestinian workers to the role of manual laborers in the Israeli economy.[5]

Palestinian laborers were drawn from the territories into the

Israeli economy much as, at an earlier stage, Israeli-Arabs living in Israel since 1948 had been drawn into employment. "A similar phenomenon took place in the early 1960's" writes a leading Israeli economist, "when an easing of restrictions inside the Israeli labor market brought about a considerable influx of temporary Arab workers from villages into the Jewish sector. It is estimated that at the height of the boom, in 1965, some 54 percent (33,000) of the total Israeli Arab male work force were employed outside their areas of normal residence."[6] Although the situation of Israeli Arabs cannot be used as a simple analogy for analyzing the possible implications of the labor situation for West Bank and Gaza Strip residents, a recent analysis of the adverse implications of commuting labor as a means of integrating Israeli Arabs into the Israeli economy is based on arguments similar to some in this study.[7]

In 1973 West Bank and Gaza Strip residents earned 581 million Israeli pounds from work in the Israeli economy.[8] This meant that by 1973, earnings in Israel accounted for some 28 percent of the gross national product of the territories. These wage earnings exceed by almost one-third the total merchandise exports from the territories.

That contrary conclusions can be drawn from the same economic facts by different observers, according to the standpoint from which they interpret the evidence, is especially evident in Israeli and Arab verdicts on the impacts of the growth of employment in Israel by residents of the territories.[9]

Israeli analysts, such as Arie Bregman of the Bank of Israel and others, offer the more positive interpretation, on a number of grounds. They note that employment opportunities in the booming Israeli economy generated fast growth in both employment and income from low starting points just after the 1967 war. They argue that much of the increased employment mobilized unemployed and underemployed elements from the potential work force. Some Israeli observers—although Bregman is more judicious in avoiding sweeping claims—conclude that there has been mutual benefit to the Israeli economy, to those employed, and to the larger economic prosperity of the two territories.

There can be no question that this phenomenon has reduced unemployment among the unskilled and semi-skilled, helped increase adult male participation in the active labor force, and provided a major source of income to residents of the territories. Nor is there any question that the process allowed the Israeli economy to sustain a considerable boom with much less pressure on the labor market than would have otherwise been the case.

There are, however, limitations inherent in this style of development, and these limitations tend to be one of the bases for critiques of Israeli economic policy, such as Jamil Hilal's.[10] Despite their much higher incomes from employment in Israel, West Bank and Gaza Strip Palestinians are the lowest-paid group in the Israeli wage structure. According to Bregman's Bank of Israel study, "Gross data indicate that a sizable gap exists between average wages paid to Israelis and the average paid to area residents working in Israel; it stood at 50 percent in 1972."[11] In 1972 the average gross monthly wage of a West Bank or Gaza Strip resident was about 500 Israeli pounds compared with 918 pounds for an Israeli.[12] Precision is difficult on this point, but other aggregate data suggest that the gap may be even wider. Figures in Table III-8 show that in 1972 the average salary per employee's post was only 384 Israeli pounds for Palestinians from the territories working in Israel. These aggregate data do not indicate whether or to what degree this overall gap results because these Palestinians are receiving less pay for the same work, or because they are concentrated in the lower paid job categories. This could only be ascertained by detailed empirical research on the nature of the work undertaken. The overall distribution of this unemployment, however, suggests that an important part of the low income levels results from occupational and industrial concentration in manual, lower paid jobs.

It is also difficult to interpret available data on deductions for health and accident insurance, and related benefits. These items are sizable, as Table III-9 indicates. Income tax by comparison is relatively unimportant: up to 25 Israeli pounds per day, it is lower for West Bank and Gaza Strip residents than for Israelis; over 25 Israeli pounds per day, there is no difference. What is ambiguous is the extent to which the territories' residents receive the same benefits as a result of these contributions as the Israelis; it is not possible to answer this question from available published data.[13] Lower access to services financed by these deductions would mean that the gap in real income derived by West Bank and Gaza Strip Palestinians from work in Israel, compared to that of Israeli workers, is even larger than suggested by the income figures alone.

The Bank of Israel study speculates about the source of the large earnings differentials between the two sets of wage-earners:

Table III-8

Number of Jobs and Amount of Salaries of Employees in Israel—Monthly Average, 1972

	Number of jobs (In thousands)	Total salary (In millions of Israeli pounds)	Average salary per employee (In Israeli pounds)
1. Including workers from the territories	911.8	814.7	893
2. Excluding workers from the territories	870.1	798.7	918
3. Workers from the territories	41.7	16.0	384

SOURCE: Data from items 1 and 2 are extracted from *Statistical Abstract of Israel 1974,* Table xii/23, p. 341. Item 3 is computed by the author from the data in items 1 and 2. This information is derived from national insurance sources and apparently has less complete coverage of the employment of area residents than other sources.

No data are available that can account for this discrepancy. It is reasonable to assume that lower training and skill levels provide part of the explanation in most branches. The difference expresses the area's excess supply of unskilled workers prepared to work for lower wages, whereas Israeli wage-earners have a wider choice of jobs, including more responsible positions within the same branch.[14]

This is a significant part of the explanation, but it could legitimately be carried further. In this situation, inevitably, the range of job opportunities for commuting Palestinian laborers will be limited by social and political factors, such as language difficulties, apprehension about security, and prejudice. Moreover, the absence of the normal citizenship rights will, in any society, limit the range of job opportunities. And Palestinian workers are likely to be in a much weaker position vis-à-vis labor organization than their Israeli counterparts. While this is likely to be particularly important in relation to job security, it may also affect the income levels enjoyed.

The significance of such factors in the long term is a matter of speculation, but the dangers inherent in the situation are clear,

Table III-9

Deductions and Employer Contributions as Percent of Gross Wage Earned in Israel by Wage-Earners from the Territories, 1972

Children's allowance	4.0	National insurance deductions and contributions*	14.9
Retraining courses	0.3	Income tax deductions	4.6
Organization dues	1.0		
Work accident insurance	2.4	Net wage	87.9
Insurance fund	24.8	Gross wage	100.0
		Total employers' labor costs	130.8

*Including employee's contribution.

SOURCE: Bregman, *Economic Growth*, p. 39.

and they are illustrated by another observation from Bregman's Bank of Israel study:"An analysis of employment rates in correlation with education levels indicates that, unlike the situation among the Jewish population of Israel, the employment rate in the administered areas goes down as the level of education (measured in years of schooling) rises. This may be attributed to the paucity of suitable jobs for educated workers. A similar problem exists among educated non-Jews in Israel, who have a relatively high unemployment rate." The situation has been alleviated insofar as the public services in the areas themselves have expanded, according to Bregman, for "the rapid increase in the employment since 1968 was particularly high among the better educated area residents (nine or more years of schooling), who were able to find employment in the areas' administrative bodies."[15]

Were it to continue, the pattern of employment which has emerged since 1967 would have controversial implications in the long term for Israel, which would be unable to avoid criticism on this matter, whichever policy it followed. If Palestinian laborers are employed in those activities in which they are most needed and acceptable in Israeli society, then Israel will be criticized for exploiting this labor. Alternatively, if this labor were excluded from employment, Israel would be charged with discrimination. And yet there is little possibility of fully integrating West Bank and Gaza Strip labor at all levels of the Israeli economy.

This dilemma is one of the main elements underlying the tricky "demographic question" that has beset the debate in Israel since 1967 about the political future of the two territories. The higher rate of natural increase among the Palestinian population augurs that the Jewish population, at some future date, might find itself in a minority if the territories remain indefinitely under Israel's jurisdiction. For example, one projection by two Israeli scholars estimates that with unchanged fertility rates and no net immigration, Arabs would outnumber Jews before the year 2000. Even making adjustments for a plausible decline in Arab fertility and a modest net rate of Jewish immigration at 15,000 per year, they judge that the Arab population would rise to 42 percent of the total by the turn of the century.[16]

Israeli apprehensions over what they refer to as the demographic question are deeply rooted and extremely complex. It is not solely a matter of arithmetic, of course. Mainstream Zionist beliefs, both before and after the creation of the state, have emphasized that a Jewish society must be built on the self-labor of Jewish workers and farmers. It would be therefore totally unacceptable ideologically for many Israelis if their country's long-term economic future were to come to depend on an Arab working class. The apprehensions are also political. Massive changes in the demography of the country would pose for Israelis agonizing choices between maintaining democratic forms in a society where the essential Jewish political majority is disappearing, or compromising them in order to maintain political control in the face of changing demography. And too, some Israelis already see the present minimal dependence on laborers from the West Bank and the Gaza Strip as a potential point of future strategic vulnerability for Israel, particularly given the tendency of these laborers to concentrate in basic industries. At the very least, what can be said is that under present political and economic circumstances none of these long-term considerations has outweighed the practical and economic advantages, in the short run, of allowing the present labor interconnections to persist.

CONSEQUENCES IN THE WEST BANK AND THE GAZA STRIP

The continuation and expansion of prevailing patterns of employment of West Bank and Gaza Strip Palestinians also could have serious consequences for the future development of the territories. The specialization would not only stifle the potential development of local managerial and professional talent, it would also generate other negative secondary effects in some sectors of the territories' economies.[17] This may be happening already. It would be surprising, even in a less tense political context, if it were not controversial.

West Bank and Gaza Strip residents working in Israel have gained economically from the expansion of employment opportunities since 1967. No doubt Israeli policies in this sphere have brought considerable economic advantage to a sizable proportion of the Palestinian population through increase in incomes, through benefits accruing to those economic activities in the territories that enjoyed an expanded market, and through the use of wage-earnings to finance some small-scale local investments. Moreover, to the balance-sheet of the economic consequences of this labor market phenomenon must be added one result of the special geographic circumstances in this particular situation. The proximity of the main centers of the Israeli economy to the normal residences of the Palestinian laborers has meant that their commuting has not had the same socially-destructive consequences witnessed in other parts of the world where the adult male population migrated over greater distances. The Palestinians from the territories who work in Israel, by contrast, live at home and maintain a normal family life, even continuing to play an economic role at home, for instance, through weekend work for the family in construction or agriculture.

The alternative against which Israel's policies during the past nine years should be judged is neither the economic situation as it existed in 1967, nor harsher Israeli policies that might have restricted income growth. More relevant would be a comparison of the actual situation with a program emphasizing more balanced expansion of employment opportunities within the West Bank and the Gaza Strip.

The attraction of such an alternative would have been that it might have mobilized Palestinian labor in the West Bank and the Gaza Strip in a way that would have expanded the basic productive capacity of their local economy, rather than transferred local employment energies to work in Israel. In this period when employment of area residents in the Israeli construction industry has grown so dramatically, investment within the territories has remained modest. In other circumstances, if finance had been avail-

Table III-10

Changes in Place of Employment of Residents of the West Bank and the Gaza Strip, 1968-74
(In Thousands)

	1968*	1969	1974	Increase or Decrease 1969-74	1968-74
Total labor force	146.5	172.8	212.5	39.7	66.0
Total employed	127.4	162.8	210.5	47.7	83.1
Employed in Israel	5.0	12.0	68.8	56.8	63.8
Employed in the West Bank and the Gaza Strip	122.4	150.8	141.7	—9.1	19.3

*Based on a slightly different statistical base, as a new sample was used from 1969 onward.

SOURCES: Bregman, *Economic Growth*, p. 29 and
Quarterly Statistics of the Administered Territories, Vol. V, No. 2 (Jerusalem: Central Bureau of Statistics, 1975).

able, and if the same labor had been employed in the West Bank and the Gaza Strip, the benefits accruing would not only have been the incomes received by the workers, but also the expansion of the local stock of buildings and other capital goods resulting from their efforts. For this to have happened, however, either a program of public investment, or conditions conducive to the expansion of private investment would have been necessary.

It is possible to argue that the transfer of West Bank and Gaza Strip labor to Israel has resulted in this kind of lost opportunity. But it is more difficult to demonstrate that there were *direct* costs to the economies of the territories as a result of this diversion.[18] Output within the West Bank and the Gaza Strip has increased, as we shall see. While there are some indications of a decline in commitment of resources to the agricultural sector— that is, some drop in acreages cultivated, no doubt because of the withdrawal of marginal land—there has been no general decline in agricultural output. (The trend in agricultural output is analyzed in Chapter 6. There have been declines in some crops and expansions in others. The net effect is difficult to ascertain; but certainly the withdrawal of labor has not caused any dramatic overall decline.) This substantial transfer of labor has been possible with-

Table III-11

Sources of Employment Growth in Israel, 1969-74

	Percent
Increase in labor force	69.9
Reduction in unemployment	14.1
Reduction in employment in the West Bank and the Gaza Strip	16.0

SOURCES: Bregman, *Economic Growth*, p. 29; and
Quarterly Statistics of the Administered Territories, Vol. V, No. 2.

out major reductions in local output because of the high early levels of unemployment and underemployment in both territories, and because the work force has grown through the natural rate of population increase. Indeed, from the immediate postwar years, 1968 to 1974, the growth of employment in Israel was accompanied by an *increase* in employment in the territories. However, 1968 is probably an unrealistic base because of the immediate disrupting effects of the war and the postwar political changes. But even taking 1969 as a base, there has been only a small drop in employment in the territories—from 150,800 in 1969 to 141,700 in 1974. (See Tables III-10 and 11.)

Labor has been available also because rising wage levels and employment opportunities have increased participation of West Bank and Gaza Strip Palestinians in the labor force. Employment of women has remained low.[19] But the male labor force participation has risen significantly. West Bank participation rates for adult males (14 years plus) rose from 56 percent in 1968 to 66.6 percent in 1973, while in the Gaza Strip the increase was from 58.8 percent to 65.7 percent. This level now corresponds roughly to the 68.5 percent participation rate in Israel. Because of the lower participation of women, the overall participation rate remains at 37.4 percent in the West Bank and 32.7 percent in the Gaza Strip in 1973.[20] (See Table III-12.) The persistence of the low participation rate overall suggests that the very low unemployment rates recorded should be interpreted cautiously, as evidence of the potential scarity of additional labor supplies if expanded local job opportunities were to exist.

Table III-12

Labor Force Characteristics of Populations in the Territories Aged 14 and Over, 1971-74

(In Thousands)

	The West Bank				The Gaza Strip and North Sinai			
	1971	1972	1973	1974	1971	1972	1973	1974
Total population	330.0	336.6	341.6	355.2	200.7	205.1	210.4	218.6
Total not in labor force	210.3	210.0	213.9	216.2	138.9	140.5	141.8	145.1
Total in labor force	119.7	126.6	127.7	139.0	61.8	64.6	68.6	73.5
Employed	116.8	125.2	126.4	137.5	59.7	63.6	68.1	73.0
Unemployed	2.9	1.4	1.3	1.5	2.1	1.0	0.5	0.5
Percent in labor force	36.3	37.6	37.4	39.1	30.8	31.5	32.6	33.6
Percent of labor force employed	97.5	98.8	98.9	98.9	96.6	98.4	99.3	99.3

SOURCE: *Statistical Abstract of Israel 1975*
(Jerusalem: Central Bureau of Statistics,
1975), Table xxvi/18, pp. 699-700.

One other important consequence of the movement of Palestinian labor into the Israeli economy has been the sharp increase in wage rates within the territories. The average daily money wage rose from 5.5 Israeli pounds in 1969 to 15.4 in 1973.[21] After allowing for the high inflation, this represented a compound growth rate in the real wage of 14 percent per annum, over a period when the real wage rate for West Bank and Gaza Strip residents employed in Israel grew 7 percent per annum. By 1973, the gap between wage rates in the Gaza Strip and for the territories' residents employed in Israel had been closed. While a significant gap in gross wages remained for West Bank residents—15.1 Israeli pounds in the West Bank compared to 21.8 pounds in Israel—in net terms, after allowing for insurance deductions, etc., the gap was by then quite small.

A rise in the real wage levels in the territories itself may indicate that the transfer of labor has been carried beyond the mobilization of workers who were previously subject to either open or hidden unemployment. Employers in the territories have had to raise wages to compete for labor with employers in Israel as labor has become scarce, confirming the judgment that some of the expansion of employment in Israel has been at the expense of employment in the territories. Interpretation of this evidence must be guarded, however. The fact of higher wage opportunities in Israel may exert a social pressure on wages in the territories, even without labor scarcity, by raising expectations of workers and changing the views of employers about acceptable wage levels. Moreover, of course, the ability to raise wages and the very need to compete for this labor are partly results of the multiplier effects of income derived from employment in Israel. But, however we judge the overall effect, the increases in wage levels as a result of competition with Israeli business in the labor market, combined with exposure to competition from Israeli goods, have created difficulties for some resident firms in the territories—difficulties that will be discussed in the next chapter.

It was not until 1972 that the level of Palestinian workers in Israel reached roughly the level of recent years. At these levels, certain features of the situation take on considerable importance. It is evident that any further growth in employment in Israel will have to be fed by reductions in employment in the West Bank and the Gaza Strip. Unemployment cannot be reduced much further and the male labor force participation rate is beginning to reach its maximum, so that the major source of manpower growth must be the underlying growth rate of the population—although some potential exists in employment of greater numbers of women and youth. Extrapolation of past trends would therefore magnify the "dormitory" features of the territories' economies at the expense of local employment.

Also, a sharp change has occurred in the structure of employment of the territories' residents. Considering their employment in Israel and the territories together, there has been a marked shift away from agriculture into construction. Thus in 1969, agriculture accounted for 50 percent of residents' employment, and construction for 11 percent; by 1973, these figures had changed to 27 percent and 21 percent respectively. Considering employment within the territories separately, however, between 1969 and 1973 there was a decline in the relative importance of both agriculture (42 percent to 31 percent) and construction (9 percent to 6 percent), with an increase in the relative importance of the service sectors (public services 12 percent to 18 percent, and trade, transport and private services, 24 percent to 30 percent) as sources of employment. In absolute terms the reduction of employment within the territories in the declining employment sectors was dramatic—from 64,000 to 40,000 in agriculture, and from 13,000 to 8,000 in construction. These shifts towards the service sector are consistent with the dominant tendency for the territories to become a dormitory economy. And, finally, achievement of these levels of Palestinian employment in Israel focuses attention on the implications of any radical changes that would disrupt the flow of laborers from the territories. The Bregman study for the Bank of Israel itself speculates on the possible buoyancy of the growth process in the absence of this stimulus, as have other studies done outside of Israel.[22] This issue is discussed in a general way in the final chapter of this study; here, it suffices only to point out that the levels of this employment have been high enough to generate attention in various quarters to the adjustment problem.

Footnotes

1. There are no official figures on the number of Palestinians who work in Israel without permits. In 1971 their numbers were estimated at 15,000 (see Vivian Bull, *The West Bank—Is it Viable?* [Lexington, Massachusetts: D. C. Heath and Co., 1975], p. 122). However, at the end of 1975 it was estimated that only 10,000 West Bank and Gaza workers commuted

to illegal jobs (see Arthur Kemelman, "Kickback Racket Led to Areas Murder," *Jerusalem Post,* January 2, 1976).

2. Those included in the three occupational classifications in Israeli labor statistics: agricultural workers; skilled workers in industry, mining, building and transport, and other skilled work; and other workers in transport and building, industry and unskilled work. For more details see *Statistical Abstract of Israel 1974* (Jerusalem: Central Bureau of Statistics, 1974), p. 305.

3. *Jerusalem Post,* December 29, 1975.

4. *Washington Post,* January 7, 1976.

5. Compare Jamil Hilal, *The West Bank: Its Social and Economic Structure (1948-1974)* (Beirut: Palestine Liberation Organization Research Center, 1975), p. 243.

6. Michael Bruno, "Economic Development of Israel, 1970-1980," in Charles A. Cooper and Sidney Alexander, eds., *Economic Development and Population Growth in the Middle East* (New York: American Elsevier, 1972), p. 105.

7. See Yosef Waschitz, "Commuters and Entrepreneurs," *New Outlook* 18 (October-November 1975): 45-53.

8. This figure is from the "labour" item in the balance of payments data in *Quarterly Statistics of the Administered Territories, Vol. IV* (Jerusalem: Central Bureau of Statistics, 1974), p. 94. This is less than the 620 million Israeli pounds which Bregman estimated based on the first three quarters of 1973 (see Arie Bregman, *Economic Growth in the Administered Areas, 1968-1973* [Jerusalem: Bank of Israel Research Department, 1975], pp. 95-97). Judging from Bregman's interpretation, this item in the balance of payments for the occupied territories only includes wages earned in Israel and does not include any estimate for residents' earnings elsewhere. The estimates seem somewhat higher than is suggested by other data on the level of employment and wages. However, this may be because the balance of payments data are based on *gross wages,* while the series of average daily wages are net wages. Using Bregman's data on the difference between these (in Table III-7 on page 39 of his book), it is possible to explain the apparent discrepancy.

9. For examples of two divergent views based upon the same set of data, see *Quarterly Statistics,* pp. 4-8; and Hilal, *op. cit.,* pp. 286-292.

10. Hilal, *op. cit.,* pp. 286-292.

11. Bregman, *op. cit.,* p. 37.

12. *Ibid.*

13. For a brief discussion see Bull, *op. cit.,* pp. 119-120; and Hilal, *op. cit.,* p. 240.

14. Bregman, *op. cit.,* pp. 37-38.

15. *Ibid.,* pp. 34-35.

16. Dov Friedlander and Calvin Goldscheider, "Peace and the Demographic Future of Israel," *Journal of Conflict Resolution* 18 (September 1974): 486-501. This study includes a number of projections under alter-

native assumptions regarding the realignment of boundaries. The areas of Sinai now returned to Egypt were included in the projections, the results of which have been quoted, but this does not affect their results in any significant way.

17. Writers sympathetic to the Palestinians make precisely this charge. For example see Hilal, *op. cit.,* pp. 239-240.

18. Hilal emphasizes that withdrawal of labor has held back the West Bank but makes his case at a general level of argument. (See Hilal, *op. cit.,* p. 243.)

19. Female employment has been rising roughly in line with total employment. For example, in the West Bank recorded female employment rose from 13,000 (15.7 percent of the total) in 1968 to 19,200 (15.2 percent of the total) in 1973. Hilal attaches some significance to this growth in female employment. See Hilal, *op. cit.,* p. 250.

20. *Statistical Abstract of Israel 1974,* p. 697.

21. Bregman, *op. cit.,* p. 37.

22. *Ibid.,* pp. 7-8. Also see for example Bull, *op. cit.,* pp. 143-152; Richard Ward, "The Economics of a Palestine Entity" in Don Peretz, Evan M. Wilson, and Richard J. Ward, *A Palestine Entity?* (Washington, D.C.: The Middle East Institute, 1970), pp. 106-114; and Elizabeth Collard and R. Wilson, *The Economic Potential of an Independent Palestine* (London: Middle East Economic Digest, 1975), *passim.*

Chapter 4

The Commodity Market

THE OVERALL PATTERN OF TRADE

Before 1967 both the West Bank and the Gaza Strip ran large deficits in visible trade. They imported a large proportion of the manufactured products used locally, and a significant percentage of their food needs. Their exports were predominantly agricultural, or processed products derived from their agricultural output, such as olive oil and oil-based soap from the West Bank.

The commodity trade between the East and West Bank before 1967 was mainly in agricultural products. The Jordanian economy, with low income levels and little industrial development, was heavily dependent upon imports as a source for most industrial products. Linkages between different branches of economic activity and between different regions were poorly developed compared to what would be expected in a more industrially advanced economy.

Since 1968, for both the West Bank and the Gaza Strip, imports have expanded faster than exports, and the basic deficit has remained. The direction of this trade, however, has changed dramatically. By 1972, merchandise exports, valued at 351 million Israeli pounds, were only 21 percent of the gross national product of 1,640 million Israeli pounds of the two territories. The direction of the export trade for 1972-73 was as follows:

West Bank and Gaza Strip 1972-73 Exports	Percent
Overseas	14
Jordan	27
Israel	58

On the other hand, imports in 1972 reached levels equal to 41 percent of the gross national product, and 31 percent of the total resources used locally. The sources of the import trade 1972-73 were as follows:

West Bank and Gaza Strip 1972-73 Imports	Percent
Overseas	10
Jordan	2
Israel	88

The current overall level of trade is indicated in Table IV-1. Two considerations need to be kept in mind when interpreting the data on the growth in trade. First, price increases have been large. No price index of foreign trade is published for the two territories, but consumer prices rose by 80 to 90 percent betwen 1968-69 and 1973. Allowing for price increases of that order in traded goods, trade almost doubled between 1968 and 1973, with a compound growth of around 14 percent per annum.[1] Second, figures for the period prior to 1968 are not available as a basis of comparison. While the growth in trading activity since then between the two territories and Israel may be somewhat exaggerated, the figures also may well underestimate the growth because the statistics do not fully record the movement of goods by individual residents in both directions.

Despite these statistical uncertainties, the emergence of trade dependence on Israel is quite clear, particularly as an import source, whereas imports from Jordan have dwindled into virtual insignificance. The export picture is somewhat different. The open bridges policy has enabled Jordan to remain a market for exports. The value of exports in current prices increased until 1972. A substantial decline in 1973 and increase in 1974 is partly explained by fluctuations in crops which are a major component of this trade. Allowing for changes in the price level, the real value of exports to Jordan does not appear to have shown any tendency to expand. Even 1972, a good export year, saw this trade reach only

Table IV-1

Balance of Trade, 1968-73
(In Millions of Israeli Pounds at Current Prices)

	The West Bank, the Gaza Strip and North Sinai combined						The West Bank		The Gaza Strip and North Sinai	
	1968	1969	1970	1971	1972	1973	1968	1973	1968	1973
Exports										
Overseas	16	22	25	57	59	59	1	2	15	57
Jordan	54	69	60	81	121	85	49	66	5	19
Israel	55	52	73	115	171	281	47	175	8	106
Total	125	143	158	253	351	425	97	243	28	182
Imports										
Overseas	39	38	44	72	84	73	20	42	19	31
Jordan	18	25	13	14	19	17	17	16	1	1
Israel	189	256	292	383	576	803	139	484	50	319
Total	246	319	349	469	679	893	176	542	70	351
Import surplus										
Overseas	23	16	19	15	25	14	19	40	4	−26
Jordan	−36	−44*	−47	−67	−102	−68	−32	−50	−4	−18
Israel	134	204	219	268	405	522	92	309	42	213
Total	121	176	191	216	328	468	79	299	42	169

SOURCE: Arie Bregman, *Economic Growth in the Administered Areas, 1968-1973* (Jerusalem: Bank of Israel Research Department), p. 84.

* This figure is shown as −34 in the original source but is corrected here.

7 percent of the West Bank and the Gaza Strip gross national product. These trends mean that while the open bridges policy helped to minimize the West Bank's economic problems in the period immediately after the 1967 war, its economic significance has declined since then. The distinguishing feature of the evolving trade pattern has been the growing West Bank and Gaza Strip trade with Israel.

TRADE WITH JORDAN

Exports from the two territories to Jordan are concentrated on a narrow range of commodities. In 1972-73, 86 percent of exports were accounted for under six headings: citrus, other fruits, vegetables, olive oil, dairy products, and West Bank soap.[2]

The structure of exports has remained basically unchanged, although some minor shifts have occurred. The relative importance of citrus has increased from 19 percent of exports in 1968 to 30 percent in 1972-73, reflecting the development of citrus exports from the Gaza Strip to the East Bank, which by 1972-1973 equaled 37,000 tons—17 percent—of total production. The olive oil trade has fluctuated with olive production. Milk products have increased in relative importance from 13 percent (1968) to 18 percent (1972-73). A number of other items have suffered a compensating decline in relative importance (*e.g.,* other fruits, vegetables, and quarried stone). Some minor items traded might be classified industrial products, such as sweets, chocolates and wafers (from Ramallah) and plastic products (from Bethlehem), but these make a very small and relatively stable contribution to the trade.

On the import side, trade with Jordan, which has declined substantially in real terms, remains largely concentrated in agricultural products or the processed products of agriculture. Paper and printed materials, films and textiles and cotton goods, although identified separately in the statistics, are of only very minor importance. Jordanian goods are subject to the Israeli external tariff on entry to the West Bank, so that the reduction in trade is hardly surprising.[3]

The net result of this largely agricultural trade between Jordan and the West Bank and the Gaza Strip is a balance of trade significantly favorable to the two territories and unfavorable to Jordan. However, too much significance should not be read into the size of this deficit. The trade is in agricultural products, sold competitively without protection. While producers on both sides of the River Jordan reap some benefit from access to convenient markets without which they would have to transport their produce over greater distances, there is neither the additional benefit to the producer from the higher prices which would result from protection, nor the additional burden on the consumer. The trade balance would be of greater significance, for example, if the commodities traded were heavily protected industrial goods.

The interesting conclusions about trade generated by the open bridges policy are mostly negative. The bridges have never been fully open in either direction: The application of Israel's tariffs to Jordan's exports, and Arab boycott restrictions intended to prevent Israeli products from moving eastward, both limit the scope of the exchange. The open bridges policy has merely maintained the trade, not expanded it. It has made no great contribution to the growth of the West Bank and the Gaza Strip, although its sudden disappearance would create transitional problems in finding alternative markets, especially for a number of local agricultural products.

This negative conclusion is of interest, however, for the light it throws upon two issues: The effect of the Arab boycott on trade with Israel, and the extent to which economic interaction of the West Bank and the Gaza Strip with the rest of the Arab world has remained limited, partly as a result of boycott restrictions.

The open bridges policy was seen by some Israelis as a potential step towards breaching the Arab boycott of trade with Israel.[4] In a direct sense, this would happen if Israeli goods were shipped on from the West Bank to Jordan, and from there to the rest of the Arab world. The available data suggest that this has not happened. All significant trade conducted across the Jordan River has continued to be in the products of the West Bank and the Gaza Strip. The Arab boycott against Israeli products has continued to be implemented by the Jordanian government. Admittedly, the possibility exists that some Israeli products, including certain agricultural items, slip through, and occasional comments by Israeli public figures call attention to this possibility; but there is little likelihood that this would be advertised in official statistics. However, the absence of growth in total trade across the Jordan and continued concentration on traditional exports which historically accounted for that trade, suggest that any breach of the boycott is trivial.[5]

The more indirect possibility is that the creation of a balance favorable to Israel in its trade with the territories, partly matched by a favorable balance in the trade between the territories and Jordan, provides a mechanism for Israel to participate in a chain of trading links extending deep into the Arab world. While this is one aspect of the situation, discussed at greater length below, its relative importance is declining.

TRADE WITH OTHER COUNTRIES

West Bank and Gaza Strip trading connections with the rest of the world, including the rest of the Arab world, have not developed since 1967, and their potential significance remains hypothetical.

Trade beyond Israel and Jordan has been limited, on the export side, to citrus produced in the Gaza Strip, and to a small volume of West Bank craft products. A miscellaneous range of goods is imported directly from overseas, almost one-half imported by "welfare institutions," including UNRWA. In all, imports from other countries fell below 10 percent of total imports by 1973. A striking characteristic of the trade picture is the extremely limited nature of the private trading connections between the territories and the outside world. No doubt, however, a significant part of the trade with Israel is, indirectly, trade with the outside world via Israel's commercial intermediaries.

Agricultural regions of the developing world characteristically have their main trading links with the more industrially developed economies rather than with other developing economies which would specialize in the production of a similar range of primary commodities. But in the Middle East, in which a number of oil producers are moving to very high income levels, the potential does exist for the development of markets, particularly for the agricultural products of the West Bank and the Gaza Strip. While some of the agricultural exports across the bridges are shipped on beyond Jordan, that potential is certainly not fully realized in the existing setting. However, the short-run prospects for trade development between the territories and the rest of the Middle East should not be exaggerated. In the immediate future such trade prospects are limited by the modest industrial base and agricultural surpluses in the territories.

TRADE WITH ISRAEL

The main trading links of the Gaza Strip and the West Bank are now with Israel. The territories have both expanded trade with Israel proper and used have Israeli trading channels as connections with the outside world.

Available data only provide a gross picture. There is neither a commodity breakdown, nor an indication of the extent to which the imports from Israel are re-exports of goods from the rest of the world. Nor is it clear whether exports to Israel are in turn re-exported. The classification of the trade between industrial and agricultural products, which is available, is not informative; the criteria for such classification are usually not very helpful for purposes of economic analysis because of the allocation, to the industrial classification, of many agricultural products that have been processed to some degree.

A number of the component elements of this growing trade can be identified, although it is not possible to rank their relative significance.

Agricultural products exported to Israel: In the early years of Israeli rule two reasons were given for restricting trade from the territories in agricultural products—to protect Israeli agriculture and to minimize security problems associated with the movement of goods. But by 1970-71 trade in agricultural products was much freer, restrictions being limited to those that protect selected crops also grown in Israel, such as dates and grapes.[6] Israeli agriculture continued to receive subsidies and minimum price guarantees not made available to agriculture in the West Bank and the Gaza Strip.[7] Nevertheless, agricultural trade did not grow dramatically. Allowing for price increases, it appears that a sharp increase occurred only in 1973.

The composition of agricultural output, to be discussed in Chapter 6, reveals little evidence that trade with Israel has substantially changed the product mix of the agricultural output of the territories. Even for the most noteworthy example—watermelon and pumpkin production, which has been reduced from 70,000 dunams to 15,000 dunams (a dunam is about one-quarter of an acre), and the land transferred to other crops—the relevant point is that in 1967-68 those products had accounted only for 4 percent of the West Bank's agricultural production. In general, crops which have expanded have been import substitutes, such as wheat and barley, plus some crops for the Israeli market. The latter have included vegetables—particularly those grown out of the Israeli—seasons and fruits, some of which are processed in Israel for shipment overseas.

Goods exported to the Arab market in Israel (which in the available data includes East Jerusalem): The Arab population of Israel, now over half a million, or almost half that of the West

Bank and the Gaza Strip, provides a market for some of the Arab specialty consumer commodities manufactured in the territories, such as chocolates, cigarettes, and soaps. Although significant for particular manufacturers, this market is not an important part of the total trade picture.

Industrial goods supplied to the Israeli market: Industry in the West Bank and the Gaza Strip, with a few notable exceptions, consists largely of small-scale enterprises which are little more than workshops, including traditional crafts of the territories— *e.g.,* carpets from Gaza, glass from Hebron, and furniture. These small firms generate an important part of the trade to Israel. There is also trade in construction materials, stone gravel and marble, produced in the West Bank quarries, and building blocks and tiles. This trade grew rapidly with the expansion of the construction industry during the Israeli boom.

There also has been a development of subcontracting by Israeli firms in the territories, concentrated mainly on the labor-intensive activities. Incidentally, this practice has provided, on a small scale, employment for Palestinian women—particularly in the clothing industry—who would not be as likely as men to commute daily to Israel.

Israeli military authorities estimated that the value of goods processed by subcontractors in the West Bank in 1972 was 6 million Israeli pounds. In that year, total industrial production was estimated by the same source as 113 million.[8] This suggests that the subcontracting system, at least until 1972, was no more than a minor part of industrial activity of the West Bank and the Gaza Strip. The entire industrial sector remains small. Industrial employment in the West Bank, including mining and quarrying, oil presses, and garages, declined from 21,000 in 1970 to 19,000 in 1972. By 1973 industrial employment was only 20,000 in the West Bank and the Gaza Strip combined (6,000 in the Gaza Strip).

Trade figures show industrial exports from the territories to Israel growing dramatically, particularly at the end of our period—rising from 145 million Israeli pounds in 1972 to 215 million in 1973 and 372 million in 1974. Bregman notes, without providing detailed statistics, that "Exports to Israel—two thirds of which originate in Judea and Samaria—consist primarily of industrial goods such as clothing and textiles, furniture, and wood products, and construction materials."[9] However, value-added in industry in the West Bank and the Gaza Strip evidently totaled 88 million Israeli pounds in 1972, and 115 million in 1973. The sales of the industries mentioned by Bregman as the major source of exports to Israel were less than one-quarter of the total sales of the industrial sector in 1972.[10] The argument that best reconciles these estimates is that the industrial trade generates relatively little local industrial income. For example, it suggests that subcontracting must result in a very modest markup. The textile and clothing trades, identified as an important component of the subcontracting trade, is the lowest paid section of West Bank and Gaza Strip industry. The figures of West Bank and Gaza Strip imports and exports are gross sales data. One hundred Israeli pounds worth of semi-manufactured imports for subcontract processing, if it generated, say, a 10 percent markup, would result in 110 Israeli pounds in industrial exports and only 10 in local income. The fast apparent growth in industrial trade has not been associated with any observable shift in the economic structure towards industry. The industrial trade figures, as currently available, should be treated cautiously as an indication of the real importance of the trading connection between Israel and the West Bank and the Gaza Strip.

In addition to subcontracting within the territories, there has been a modest effort to set up industrial activities near the Gaza Strip border at the Eretz industrial estate, which by 1973 had attracted thirteen Israeli enterprises, employing over 300 workers from the territory.

Israeli and Palestinian commentaries do not attribute the same significance to this subcontracting.[11] Bregman stresses how this type of development is widely advocated as an appropriate strategy in low income countries, implying perhaps that subcontracting is envisaged as playing an increasingly important role in the territories. However, as the wage differential for Palestinian labor narrows between the territories and Israel, the incentive to subcontract labor rather than to employ Palestinians in workshops in Israel will be reduced. The remaining incentive is likely to be the lower insurance and similar payments, plus the possibility of more readily utilizing female labor.

On the other hand, subcontracting has some of the same short-term economic advantages and disadvantages as the more important phenomenon of the transfer of unskilled labor directly to the Israeli economy. And in the long term, the economic success of the process depends partly on whether subcontracting creates the experience and skills needed to exploit future opportunities in local or export markets, or whether it merely perpetu-

Table IV-2

Israel Exports: 1966-73
(In Thousands of Dollars)

	Gross exports	Exports (Net exports to the West Bank and the Gaza Strip)	Exports to the West Bank and the Gaza Strip as per-cent of gross exports
1966	503,444	503,444	
1967	569,000	554,453	2.6
1968	690,062	639,219	7.4
1969	797,240	729,310	8.5
1970	852,587	778,735	8.7
1971	1,059,982	957,609	9.7
1972	1,284,020	1,146,972	10.7
1973	1,637,159	1,448,659	11.5

SOURCE: *Statistical Abstract of Israel 1974*
(Jerusalem: Central Bureau of Statistics,
1974), p. 198.

ates the less-desirable aspects of the existing Palestinian labor situation, emphasizing the supply of unskilled labor to the external market, a dilemma acknowledged by Bregman:

> The proof of the system's usefulness could be in the replacement of sub-contracting jobs with the full production of the same products. This would most probably call for measures to protect at least part of the administered areas' domestic production from competition by Israeli products—as is common for infant industries. It would also require finding new export outlets. [12]

Imports from Israel: As this quotation implies, the dominant element of the new trading pattern has been the opening of the markets of the West Bank and the Gaza Strip to Israeli products. The most striking feature of the trade figures is the deficit with Israel, which by 1973 had reached 522 million Israeli pounds. This large negative item was balanced by positive contributions in other sections of the balance of payments, including the large positive balance in the services account generated by wages earned in Israel, the positive balance on the trade account with Jordan, remittances from residents working outside areas controlled by Israel, and the expenditures of the Israeli government in the territories.

Israel's exports to the West Bank and the Gaza Strip have grown enough to become a significant element in the overall Is-

Table IV-3

Israel Major Export Markets
(In Thousands of Dollars)

	1971	1972	1973
Total Exports	1,059,982	1,284,020	1,637,159
The West Bank and			
the Gaza Strip	102,373	137,048	188,500
The United States	185,548	223,473	267,009
The United Kingdom	97,515	111,249	140,799
West Germany	90,585	103,645	137,650
The Netherlands	57,875	67,439	97,960
Hong Kong	45,268	60,889	96,943
Others	480,818	580,277	708,298

SOURCE: Adapted from *Statistical Abstract of Israel 1974*, pp. 198, 209, and 210.

raeli export situation. By 1973, when the relative importance of this trade reached a peak, 12 percent of Israel's net exports went to the two territories; 17 percent of the growth in Israeli exports between 1966 and 1973 was accounted for by the existence of this market. By 1973 the only national market more important to Israel than this was the U.S. market. In that year, Israeli exports to the territories were 803 million Israeli pounds, that is, about $178-191 million worth of goods,[13] while exports to the United States were $267 million. Tables IV-2 and IV-3 provide more detailed information on the growth and pattern of Israel's trade. However, it should be noted that these earnings only represent foreign exchange gains to Israel insofar as the West Bank and Gaza Strip finance Israeli imports through their earnings from the rest of the world, including Jordan. It is also true that insofar as some unidentifiable part of this export trade relates to the subcontracting industry, and as such is returned to Israel, the importance of the market is exaggerated by the data.

TRADE BETWEEN THE GAZA STRIP AND THE WEST BANK

Comprehensive data are not available on the growth of trade between the Gaza Strip and the West Bank. Because no special effort has been made to encourage such trade, and because the range of industrial goods produced in both territories is very limited, there is no reason to suppose that such trade has yet become significant.

Information on part of the trade in agricultural produce indicates that the Gaza Strip has established a modest market in the West Bank and Jordan, particularly for the sale of citrus, the leading product of that area. The Gaza Strip sells about 5 percent of its total fruit and vegetable production to the West Bank. On the other hand, the West Bank exports very few agricultural products to the Gaza Strip. Israel, however, has been a significant source of supply for fruit and vegetables in both areas. By 1972-73 Israel supplied almost one-fifth (by weight) of the food and vegetables consumed in the two territories.[14] This trade, though not large, indicates that the main expansion of trading links has been between Israel and the two territories respectively, rather than between the two territories themselves. Accelerated development of trading links between the West Bank and the Gaza Strip would require the support of active policies. It is the absence of such policies that is conspicuous.

IMPLICATIONS OF THE TRADING PATTERN

Although a specific calculation of the costs and returns of the trading pattern is not possible because the detailed commodity breakdown of the export trade from Israel to the territories is not known, the general pattern of trade can be discussed. It is relevant to view this pattern against the background of what is known about the dynamics of common markets and custom unions.

Participants derive benefits from a common trading arrangement insofar as exports can be expanded at higher prices than would have been possible without the arrangement. They incur costs if imports are diverted from lower to higher priced sources of supply. If the arrangement generates increased efficiency through greater specialization resulting from increased trading possibilities, all may benefit.

For underdeveloped economies special considerations apply. They often attempt to change their pattern of specialization, for example, by protecting infant industries or by subsidizing non-traditional exports. From the point of view of a less-developed trading partner, therefore, the arrangement is judged not only for its immediate efficiency but also for whether it allows or limits the desired basic changes in trade and economic structure.

From this perspective, two features of Israeli trade links with the West Bank and the Gaza Strip are crucial. On the one hand, by buying Israeli products or overseas products imported through Israel, the Palestinians in the territories are subject to the effects of the Israeli external tariff. On the other hand, trade between Israel and the territories has been restricted only to protect Israeli agriculture, either by limiting the flow of agricultural produce into Israel or by subsidizing Israeli agricultural production.

For the territories' residents, this relationship has important implications. Insofar as some goods now imported from Israel previously came from a source with similar or higher prices, no immediate cost is involved. There may even be some advantages if protected Israeli goods are displacing equally or more highly protected goods otherwise supplied by Jordan or if Israeli goods are priced to meet open competition in the world market.

However, Israeli industry is heavily protected. Where Israeli goods are not competitive in the world market and are able to be sold in the West Bank and the Gaza Strip merely because of the level of protection, then the residents bear a cost determined by the level of effective protection.

The gross magnitude of nominal protection is indicated by the average payment by the importer compared to the value of the imports. For 1972 these figures were:

Ratio of Importer Payment to
Value of Imports (1972)*

All Imports	1.28
Consumer Goods	1.64
Non Durable	1.37
Foods	1.21
Durable	2.11
Production Inputs	1.20
Investment Goods	1.30

These ratios suggest that the gap was considerable. The level of protection on consumer goods is particularly high, allowing an average Israeli producer to sell at prices almost two-thirds above the import prices. As productive inputs are protected at a much lower rate, the level of effective protection, that is, of value added

---

*This has been calculated from Table viii/12 in *Statistical Abstract of Israel 1974 (Jerusalem: Central Bureau of Statistics, 1974)*, p. 219, by dividing the average payments by importer per dollar in Israeli pounds by the exchange rate ($1 = 4.20). This ratio measures the total effect of custom duty, surcharges, purchase tax and funds.

in the final stages of manufacturing, is even higher than is suggested by these ratios. A cost is imposed on the Palestinian consumers in the West Bank and the Gaza Strip, who have to share the same burden as Israeli consumers, while Israeli producers gain access to highly protected markets.

When goods traded do not originate in Israel but are overseas commodities transferred, the territories' residents bear a cost in the form of duties levied on entry of the commodities into Israel. Of course, since duties would normally be levied on some of these imports in any circumstances, there is only a cost to the economy as a whole insofar as this fiscal burden is not matched by corresponding expenditures in the territories, as discussed in the next chapter.

Trade in the other direction—sales of commodities from the West Bank and the Gaza Strip to Israel—reached 280 million Israeli pounds by 1973, equal to 13 percent of the gross national product of the territories. This was a sizable market, even though it equaled just less than half the value of wages earned by the Palestinian residents in Israel. However, part of this trade, as we noted above, is in agricultural products competing in the Israeli market with the output of Israeli agriculture which is subsidized. The West Bank and Gaza Strip producers selling under such conditions in the Israeli market would not benefit to the same degree as Israeli producers selling the more highly protected range of manufactured goods.

Most imports from Israel to the two territories are broadly classified as industrial goods—83 percent in 1972-73—and most are for private consumption.[15] This suggests that there may be a heavy concentration on those commodities which are particularly highly protected—that is, consumer goods, for which the gross level of protection was 64 percent in 1972. This does not tell us, of course, that Israeli goods actually sold in these categories were that much more expensive than foreign products.

The remaining part of this chapter evaluates the consequences of this pattern of trade. It should be noted that the trading connections are part of the total set of economic interrelationships being analyzed. In particular, from the Israeli point of view, the employment of labor from the West Bank and Gaza Strip is only possible because of the compensating positive trade balance that Israel enjoys with the two territories. That is, if the wages earned by West Bank and Gaza Strip residents in Israel were spent on imports from the rest of the world, then Israel would be unable to sustain the balance of payments costs of that employment and would either have to reduce its amount or cut the level of real wages paid. Evaluation of the trading links therefore should be considered alongside the discussion of the labor market links in the previous chapter.

Considered in itself, the overall pattern of post-1967 trade interconnections summarized in Table IV-4 suggests several conclusions.

First, the trade in commodities has generated a significant, heavily protected market for Israeli products, and the market played a surprisingly large role in the expansion of Israeli exports in 1967-73. We have no means of judging how much of this trade would continue in the absence of favored access, if Israeli producers competed on an equal basis with other foreign suppliers.

Second, this advantage enjoyed by Israeli producers imposed a cost on the territories' residents; on the other side of the balance sheet, but to a much more limited degree, some Palestinian producers benefited from the access to the Israeli market. The shift in the direction and nature of trade must have had considerable consequences for the traders of the West Bank and the Gaza Strip, an important segment of the business community. Hilal has argued that the trading bourgeois has benefited from the new pattern of growth.[16] Independent empirical evidence to assess that judgment is not available. But the overall expansion in commercial activity resulting from accelerated economic growth must have provided ample opportunities for traders to shift to new lines of activity and to establish positions in the web of new trading connections. It may also be reasoned, however, that some segments of the trading community must have been faced with difficulties. Those in the overseas import-export business, for example, must have found their positions threatened as trade shifted to Israeli trading channels.

Third, there has been an erosion of the position of Jordan in the trading picture, and an absence of the development of trading links with other parts of the Middle East.

Fourth, whatever the immediate costs and benefits of the trading pattern, there are also long-term consequences on the trading relationship for the industrial structure of the West Bank and the Gaza Strip. If the present trends persist, the absence of tariff protection from Israeli competition, or other forms of government support, will mean that local industry is only likely to develop when it plays a role complementary to Israeli industry. In

Table IV-4 (1 of 3)

Balance of Payments: West Bank and Gaza Strip

(In Millions of Israeli Pounds at Current Prices)

C = Credit; D = Debit

	1968						1969					
	With Israel		With rest of the world		Total		With Israel		With rest of the world		Total	
	C	D	C	D	C	D	C	D	C	D	C	D
Total goods and services	82	220	101	86	183	306	113	310	105	85	218	395
Goods	55	189	70	57	125	246	52	256	91	63	143	319
Services	27	31	31	29	58	60	61	54	14	22	75	76
Transport services		1		5		6		10				10
Insurance		1				1	1	2		1	1	3
Travel abroad	15	13	24	23	39	36	8	13	9	21	17	34
Income from investments			4		4			8	3		3	8
Government	12	8	3	1	15	7	52	10	2		54	10
Labor		1				9		11				11
Other						1						
Unilateral transfers	74		108	1	182	1	76		129	12	205	12
Private unilateral transfers			108	1	108	1			129	12	129	12
Israel government	74				74		76				76	
Total net capital movements	64		—	122		58	121		—	137		16

SOURCE: Bregman, Economic Growth, Table V-1, pp. 80-81; and Table V-6, p. 91.
The columns for the "rest of the world" are derived by subtracting the Israel figures from the total.

Table IV-4 (2 of 3)

Balance of Payments: West Bank and Gaza Strip

(In Millions of Israeli Pounds at Current Prices)

C = Credit; D = Debit

| | 1970 | | | | | | 1971 | | | | | |
| | With Israel | | With rest of the world | | Total | | With Israel | | With rest of the world | | Total | |
	C	D	C	D	C	D	C	D	C	D	C	D
Total goods and services	192	371	99	78	291	449	340	505	166	105	506	610
Goods	73	292	85	57	158	349	115	383	138	86	253	469
Services	119	79	14	21	133	100	225	122	28	19	253	141
Transport services		11		2		13		17		2		19
Insurance	3	5	1	1	4	6	5	6	3	3	8	9
Travel abroad	5	10	7	16	12	26	10	12	14	12	24	24
Income from investments			3		3	0			3	1	3	1
Government		10				10		11				11
Labor	111	12	3		114	12	210	16	8	2	218	18
Other		31		2		33		60		-1		59
Unilateral transfers	88		158	18	246	18	112		144	30	256	30
Private unilateral transfers			158	18	158	18			144	30	144	30
Israel government	88				88		112				112	
Total net capital movements	91		—	161	—	70	53		—	175	112	122

Table IV-4 (3 of 3)

Balance of Payments: West Bank and Gaza Strip

(In Millions of Israeli Pounds at Current Prices)

C = Credit; D = Debit

	1972 With Israel		1972 With rest of the world		1972 Total		1973 With Israel		1973 With rest of the world		1973 Total	
	C	D	C	D	C	D	C	D	C	D	C	D
Total goods and services	595	733	240	164	835	897	928	1,017	178	155	1,106	1,172
Goods	171	576	197	117	368	693	281	803	157	97	438	900
Services	424	157	43	47	467	204	647	214	21	58	668	272
Transport services		26	4	3	4	29	21	25	-16	12	5	37
Insurance	6	7	1	5	7	12	4	12	4	4	8	16
Travel abroad	12	14	22	29	34	43	13	13	18	51	31	64
Income from investments		10	3	1	3	11			4	1	4	1
Government	406	10	13	3	419	13	609	17	11	1	620	18
Labor		90		6		96		47		77		124
Other									0	12	0	12
Unilateral transfers	141		149	62	290	62	172		164	58	336	58
Private unilateral transfers			149	62	149	62			164	58	164	58
Israel government	141				141		172		—		172	
Total net capital movements		3		163		166		17				212

the extreme case, in relation to some agricultural products, the subsidization of Israeli producers makes it particularly difficult for Palestinian producers to compete. The result does provide an immediate benefit to local consumers—but at the expense of damaging local production.

Fifth, the limited development of local industrial production is a result of factors relating not only to trade policy but also to the lack of movement of capital into the two territories. This is not to say that indiscriminate movement of capital into the West Bank and the Gaza Strip would be desirable. But taken alongside the movement of labor into Israel and the free movement of Israeli commodities into the West Bank and the Gaza Strip, the limited availability of either private or public industrial investment funds, seemingly inherent in the existing situation, leaves the prospects for local industrial growth very dim. Even with protection or other support, comprehensive industrialization could not be readily achieved. The economies are small and natural resources limited. Any claim that there is a swift and straightforward path to industrialization would be naive. However, any government concerned with the long-term needs of the two territories would concern itself with the selective development of industry, seeking to develop some expertise in new lines of industrial endeavor for the local and export market—much as Israel did with its own industries. Despite the high rates of growth generated particularly by employment in Israel, the local economies have been marking time both before and after 1967, and options for the development of a more balanced economic structure have not been tested with any determination.

Footnotes

1. Bregman suggests a real rate of increase of 10 percent annually for the West Bank and 35 percent for the Gaza Strip; see Arie Bregman, *Economic Growth in the Administered Areas, 1968-1973* (Jerusalem: Bank of Israel Research Department, 1975), p. 79.

2. Since the standard trade classification counts olive oil, soap, and dairy products as "industrial exports," the aggregate data can be misleading. For example, in 1972 just over one-half of the exports to Jordan were recorded as "industrial exports," but four-fifths were those three items, which are no more than the processed products of the agricultural sector. Both Bregman (*op. cit.,* p. 93) and Hilal (Jamil Hilal, *The West*

Bank: Its Social and Economic Structure (1948-1974) [Beirut: Palestine Liberation Organization Research Center, 1975], p. 226) overemphasize the industrial character of this trade.

3. Vivian Bull, *The West Bank—Is It Viable?* (Lexington, Massachusetts: D. C. Heath and Co., 1975), pp. 51-53.

4. See the prologue, p. 16ff., *supra.*

5. Nevertheless, from time to time there are reports that Israeli products—minus labels of origin—find their way across the bridges. For example, see Francis Ofner, "Israel-Jordan Unofficial Trade Flourishes," *Christian Science Monitor,* December 30, 1975.

6. See Bregman, *op. cit.,* p. 51; and Dani Tzidkoni, "Colonial Policy in the Territories," *New Outlook* 18 (July-August 1975): 41-42. For some Israeli farmers, however, the protection has seemed inadequate—as suggested by their occasional demonstrations against West Bank agricultural imports, including an instance in 1975.

7. Hilal emphasizes the negative impact of these subsidies on agriculture in the West Bank, claiming that poultry and dairy production in particular suffer from subsidized Israeli competition; *op. cit.,* p. 247.

8. Coordinator of Government Operations in the Administered Territories, *The Administered Territories, 1972/1973* (Yaffo, Israel: Ministry of Defence, n.d.), pp. 89-90. What concept of industrial production is used here is unclear. The statistics in this document are fragmentary and seem to be the by-product of the supervisory activities of the military administration, rather than systematic statistical collection. In the absence of other data, however, this is some indication of the relative importance of this activity.

9. Bregman, *op. cit.,* p. 93.

10. *Ibid.,* p. 89.

11. *Ibid.,* p. 4; and Hilal, *op. cit.,* p. 250.

12. Bregman, *op. cit.,* p. 84.

13. Depending on whether the official exchange rate (4.20 Israeli pounds to the dollar) or the black market rate (4.50 to the dollar) is used.

14. *Statistical Abstract of Israel 1974* (Jerusalem: Central Bureau of Statistics, 1974), p. 709.

15. Bregman, *op. cit.,* p. 93. Note that the argument offered about the misleading nature of such broad classifications also applies here—some undisclosed part of this "industrial" trade will be processed agricultural products.

16. Hilal, *op. cit.,* pp. 301-302.

Chapter 5

Financial Links

Of all the economic interconnections between the West Bank and the Gaza Strip and neighboring economies, the monetary and fiscal links are both the most difficult to describe from published sources and the most difficult to interpret. These links have produced a complex and ambiguous situation because the considerable degree of continuity before and after 1967 is not fully documented, and such change as there has been must be inferred from other economic developments discussed in this study.

The Israeli occupation resulted in the disruption of the existing monetary and banking systems without establishing a fully-fledged alternative. The West Bank, in particular, was left in an unusual situation. Existing commercial banks ceased operation, but were not more than marginally replaced by Israeli alternatives. Nevertheless, the Jordanian dinar continued to circulate alongside the Israeli pound, so that in effect the West Bank economy operated as part of two monetary systems—that of Israel and that of Jordan—but with inadequate commercial banking facilities.

In the fiscal sphere, much of the pre-1967 structure of public finance has remained in operation. But the increasing connections with the Israeli economy began to modify significantly the incidence of taxation borne by the Palestinians in the territories. In the monetary sphere of the West Bank and the Gaza Strip, residents have been exposed to the Israeli monetary system and through it to the steep inflation experienced in recent years by the Israeli economy. For both spheres, it is possible to piece together a satisfactory picture of the way the system works and of its principal effects.

FISCAL ARRANGEMENTS

Within the West Bank and the Gaza Strip, the Israeli authorities retained the pre-1967 system of taxation, with average levels of taxation much lower than in Israel. However, the Palestinian residents were affected by fiscal changes arising from certain features of economic life in the two territories. In particular:

(a) West Bank and Gaza Strip workers in Israel have been subject to payroll deductions, as described in Chapter 3, for those earning 25 Israeli pounds per day, at levels equal to those experienced by Israeli workers and at somewhat lower rates for those earning less than 25 pounds per day;

(b) consumers in the West Bank and the Gaza Strip have had to bear the burden of Israeli duties on goods imported through Israel, and of those taxes on Israeli products they consume whose incidence falls on the consumer; and

(c) the Jerusalem residents after annexation in 1967 became liable to higher Israeli taxes.

Since 1967, revenues directly accruing to the public sector in the territories have been persistently lower than expenditures, the balance being met from military government sources, particularly in the Gaza Strip, where the local revenue base is very small. Public sector expenditures have expanded somewhat more slowly than the gross national product of the territories,[1] and slower than the revenues collected. The contributions of the military government have declined substantially relative to total expenditures, from 72 percent in 1968-69 to 56 percent in 1972-73. (See Table V-1.)

It has been a persistent concern in Israel that military rule over the West Bank and the Gaza Strip should not become a serious financial burden.[2] In practice it is difficult to estimate whether Israeli contributions to the budget of the territories represents a net fiscal transfer. The difficulty arises from uncertainty about the size of the revenues accruing indirectly to the Israeli government, as a result of the economic activities of the West Bank and Gaza Strip residents. Bregman recognizes this difficulty and suggests that "there are different estimates of the 'budget burden' for 1968-73.'' He points out that there are various ways and means of arriving at these estimates, which range between 300 and 700 million Israeli pounds at 1971 prices.[3]

This is fair enough. But whatever the net burden was, it has changed sharply as the economic activities of the territories' residents have expanded. The following figures demonstrate why:

	1968-69	1972-73
	In Millions of Israeli Pounds	
Financing from the military government	67	126
Negative trade balance with Israel	119	464
Labor income (averages of 1968 and 1969, 1972 and 1973) in Israel	32	509
Total flows providing tax base in Israel	151	973

Using these figures as a rough index, it seems likely that in 1968-69 there was a substantial net transfer by Israel—but still not more than a very minor item in the Israeli national budget. Net trade and employment incomes of West Bank and Gaza Strip Palestinians would have had to generate tax at an average rate of 44 percent to have balanced the military government financing. By 1972-73 the picture had changed: the net trade balance and employment income needed to generate tax take through both direct and indirect means at a rate of only 13 percent to compensate for the military government's contribution. The tax take must have been considerably higher than that, given Israeli tax rates, and even allowing for the possibility that only a portion should be ascribed to the two territories. (It could be argued, for example, that some part of the income tax *should* accrue to the authority where the worker is employed rather than where he resides.) Thus the macroeconomic data strongly suggest that by 1972-73 the West Bank and the Gaza strip were no longer in fiscal deficit and, under perfectly plausible assumptions, they could well have been in fiscal surplus vis-à-vis Israel.

Table V-1

Public Sector Financing, 1968/69-1972/73
(In Millions of Israeli Pounds at Current Prices)

	The West Bank					
	1966	1968/ 69	1969/ 70	1970/ 71	1971/ 72	1972/ 73
A. Revenues						
Direct taxes	9	1	2	2	5	7
Indirect taxes	55	22	35	43	57	70
Other revenues	6	2	3	3	4	9
Total	70	25	40	48	66	86
B. Expenditure						
Consumption*	97***	51	56	65	83	109
Investment	13	13	19	20	20	26
Transfers and subsidies		2	3	2	2	3
Total	110	66	78	87	105	138
C. Excess demand (B—A)	40	41	38	39	39	52
D. Net credit, errors and omissions**		—3	—2	1	1	0
E. Financing from military government		38	36	40	40	52

*Current purchases minus sales, excluding defense
expenditures and the penitentiary service which
are defined as part of Israel's public consumption.

**Residual item.

***Of which some 50 million Israeli pounds are for
defense expenditures.

Israeli official sources themselves tend to emphasize that the civil operation of the West Bank and the Gaza Strip has not been a great fiscal burden.[4] Bregman suggests that after allowing for tax revenues accruing in Israel and subsidies it is possible to justify an estimate of the budget burden for the period 1968-73 in the range between 300 million and 700 million Israeli pounds at 1971 prices.[5] The argument developed above suggests that it was at the bottom of that range and the "fiscal burden" was concentrated in the early years.

Given that the Israeli budget for the West Bank and Gaza Strip does not include any defense expenditures, and that there

The Gaza Strip					
	1966	1968/ 69	1969/ 70	1970/ 71	1971/ 72	1972/ 73

	1966	1968/69	1969/70	1970/71	1971/72	1972/73
A. Revenues						
Direct taxes	3	1	1	1	1	3
Indirect taxes	19	2	3	4	7	15
Other revenues	2	1	2	2	2	2
Total	24	4	6	7	10	20
B. Expenditure						
Consumption*	24	19	25	34	43	55
Investment	3	4	15	16	19	26
Transfers and subsidies		4	2	3	3	5
Total	27	27	42	53	65	86
C. Excess demand (B—A)	3	23	36	46	55	66
D. Net credit, errors and omissions**		6	2	0	6	8
E. Financing from military government		29	38	46	61	74

SOURCE: Arie Bregman, *Economic Growth in the Administered Areas, 1968-1973* (Jerusalem: Bank of Israel Research Department, 1975), p. 74.

has been a low level of public investment and no dramatic expansion of public services, it would not be surprising if the two territories have by now reached hypothetical fiscal surplus when estimated indirect revenues are accounted for, after a period of fast economic growth.

Thus, by 1972-73 the residents of the West Bank and the Gaza Strip may well have been making a net contribution to the Israeli budget. This suggests that, with the available taxable capacity, higher levels of public services and investment could have been maintained in the territories. Or alternatively, it suggests that in the event of any political change causing a decline in economic activity, the overall burden of maintaining the public services would not be as onerous as if services had been expanded in line with economic growth.

One aspect of the fiscal situation of the West Bank not clarified in published statistics is the continuing role played by the government of Jordan. That the role is being played is not seriously doubted; it is not certain how large a role it is, or how widely it has fluctuated over time. After 1967 the Jordanian government continued to pay the salaries and pensions of some categories of public servants. Also, financing for some development projects has been made available to West Bank municipalities after the projects have been approved by the Israeli military government. These practices have been of obvious political importance in maintaining Jordanian contacts and influence in the West Bank. As the level of public investment has evidently remained low, with municipalities implementing mainly small-scale projects on the basis of this Jordanian funding, the economic importance of the development subventions has not been great. There is insufficient evidence to evaluate the total economic importance of these remaining fiscal connections between the West Bank and Amman.

THE MONETARY SYSTEM

Before 1967, the commercial bank branches in the West Bank and the Gaza Strip had been either Arab banks or the British-owned bank, largely those doing business throughout the Middle East. Jordanian currency and Egyptian currency circulated in the West Bank and the Gaza Strip respectively.

In the immediate aftermath of the 1967 war the commercial banks were closed. The Israeli authorities were unwilling to allow the commercial bank branches to reopen and operate under control of their head offices in Amman.[6] Subsequent negotiations to reopen the banks have foundered on the failure of Israel and the banking authorities to agree on principles of operation. Two issues at stake have been the control of branches in the West Bank by headquarters in Amman and the reopening of branches in East Jerusalem, both unacceptable to Israel.

An account of the negotiations about this issue, and the precise terms of the disagreement, is not publicly available. However, the consequences of the closure of the commercial bank branches are clear and are the main interest here. As the inactive banks have been replaced only to a very minor degree by Israeli commercial banks, economic transactions in the territories have been carried on without normal access to banking facilities. This is one reason, of course, for the paucity of data on the monetary situation.

In 1967, commercial bank assets and liabilities were estimated to be worth 14 million Jordanian dinars in the West Bank. The Jordanian authorities saw their deposits as both a moral and legal liability of the headquarters of the banks. However, the assets (mortgages, etc.) were to a considerable extent located in the branches, and not under the control of the head offices. Customers repaying outstanding debts to the head offices would be in jeopardy, because hypothetically the Israeli authorities could have asserted that the liability to the branch was still outstanding, not recognizing transactions conducted with head offices in Amman.

Jordan's response to this anomalous situation was initially to freeze the liabilities of the banks, subsequently allowing deposits to be withdrawn at a pace that did not undermine the liquidity of the Jordanian banking system. To make this possible an estimated 3.4 million Jordanian dinars of central bank liquidity were provided. By mid-1975 about 80 percent of the deposits had been paid out, leaving about 2 million Jordanian dinars outstanding. On the asset side of the account about 30 percent of outstanding debts were collected, repayment being specially concentrated in those instances where the headquarters of the commercial banks held bills in Amman. No effort had been made by the Jordanian authorities to enforce repayments of debts to the Industrial and Agricultural Development Banks, which are public development finance institutions.

Israeli banks have opened branches in the territories, but they have not succeeded in establishing themselves. By the end of 1972 sixteen Israeli branches—about half the total number of pre-1967 bank branches—held total public deposits of 75 million Israeli pounds. The Bank of Israel estimates that deposits in banks amount to only "4 percent of product as against 29 percent before the war (1966)."[7]

According to the Bank, the Israeli commercial banks make few loans in the territories; as a consequence, deposits by the Palestinian population are channeled into the Israeli economy. As the Israeli banks have not succeeded in expanding their business greatly, this is not of great importance. But it would become more so if the banks become the normal recipients of the savings and cash holdings of the territories' residents.

The opportunities for the West Bank Palestinians to maintain a degree of independence from the Israeli monetary system were increased by the continuing circulation of the Jordanian dinar. After an initial period when Israel considered the possibility of completely replacing the Jordanian dinar, the dinar was allowed to continue circulating as legal tender alongside the Israeli pound. This facilitated both the recovery of business activity within the West Bank and the restoration of trade across the River Jordan.

Faced with a choice between holding dinars or Israeli pounds, the local population has retained a preference for holding Jordanian dinars. Given the solid record of the dinar as a relatively stable, hard currency as against the Israeli pound, with its record of continuing and substantial depreciation, this would be a perfectly understandable preference, apart from any traditional or political attachment.[8] Indeed, since the Jordanian dinar is relatively freely available to Israelis, it would not be surprising if Israeli citizens themselves hold dinars.

Furthermore, the acceptance of the continuing circulation of dinars and of the role of moneychangers as dealers in foreign exchange outside the normal banking system must have involved some serious costs for the Israeli monetary authorities, as it provided a significant loophole in the Israeli exchange control arrangements. Recent official efforts to control the moneychangers indicates that this has been a source of official concern.

As a result of the limited use made of Israeli commercial banks it seems that the Palestinians in the territories either keep their money holdings in the form of cash or bank it outside the territories and Israel. Transactions are facilitated by the operation of the moneychangers, who operate on a much larger scale than would be likely if the banking system were fully operative.

The outcome of these developments was a very considerable decline in commercial bank activity.[9] What is most distinctive about the resulting situation is that the expanded economic activities of the West Bank and the Gaza Strip are therefore sustained largely by cash transactions and that the cash in circulation in the West Bank continues to include substantial quantities of Jordanian dinars.

The initial source of this supply of Jordanian money in the West Bank was the cash in circulation in 1967. Subsequent transactions will have changed this stock. A notable inflow has resulted from the favorable trade balance across the Jordan River. Whether other financial transactions by West Bank residents had any net effect on the availability of dinars is not possible to estimate. Some inflow may have been due to remittances from family members working in the East Bank and elsewhere and to transfers from liquidation of deposits with Jordanian banks in Amman. There may also have been transfers outwards from the territories, for investment purposes, or into bank accounts maintained beyond Israeli jurisdiction. For example, there appears to have been significant West Bank investment in Amman real estate. Indeed, in 1974 the Jordanian authorities took steps to control this practice because of its speculative effects.

Some of the dinars are continually exchanged for Israeli pounds. The Israeli authorities provide a favorable exporters' exchange rate for dinars earned in the Jordanian export trade in order to gain access to a strong foreign currency. The negative trade balance between the two territories and Israel itself requires some exhange of dinars for Israeli pounds to finance imports from Israel and overseas into the West Bank.

The likelihood is that in recent years the Palestinians of the West Bank and the Gaza Strip have accumulated an increasing stock of liquid assets; as incomes have risen, savings will have risen also, while attitudes have remained cautious in relation to capital investments probably partly because of political uncertainties. Given the limited use of bank accounts, it therefore seems possible that there is substantial cash hoarding, which would also be consistent with currency needs for normal economic transactions in a monetary system without active commercial banks.

The precise quantity of Jordanian dinars circulating in the West Bank cannot be definitely established. The Bregman study suggests that the "means of payment" (concept undefined) is about "half of product," without stating the basis for the estimate (presumably Bregman means national product). This would suggest that the total money supply in the territories would have a value equivalent to 40-45 million Jordanian dinars, some of which would be in the form of Israeli pounds. On the other hand, Jordanian sources offered the "guestimate" in 1975 that 40-50 million Jordanian dinars alone are in circulation in Israeli-held territory. Some of these might be held, of course, in Israel itself. A figure of 40 million as a rough order of magnitude, therefore, seems in line with Israeli and Jordanian estimates of the total circulation of Jordanian dinars in Israeli-held territory.

The total issue of Jordanian dinars held by the public, in Jordan and elsewhere, was at a level of 115 million by the end of 1974; the total money supply, including demand deposits, was 170 million. Taking the estimate of 40 million as a guide, more than a third of Jordanian currency and as much as one-quarter of the Jordanian money supply are circulating in Israeli-held territory. Even if these figures are only approximate, it is obvious that substantial amounts are involved.

This monetary situation illuminates the complexity of the pattern of economic interconnections that has emerged. Despite a high degree of involvement in the Israeli economy through both the labor and commodity markets, the economies of the territories, and of the West Bank in particular, have not been assimilated into the Israeli monetary system. Continuing access to the Jordanian dinar has been of considerable value to the West Bank residents, as it has provided them with alternative monetary holdings to the swiftly depreciating Israeli pound. Whether for reasons of commercial prudence or political choice, the penetration by Israeli commercial banks has been limited, the circulation of the Jordanian dinar continues and financial links are maintained with Amman. This, indeed, stands as the principal exception to the prevalent pattern since 1967, which has been one of progressively deeper interpenetration of major sectors of the West Bank and Gaza Strip economies with the Israeli economic system.

For Jordanian authorities, the circulation of a substantial part of their money supply in a region outside their control poses interesting questions. On the one hand, Jordan's short-term interest is served by the willingness of West Bankers to hold the dinar: this is not dissimilar from their supplying a loan to the Jordan economy. As a result of West Bankers holding, or using within the West Bank economy, the dinars acquired in trade with the East Bank, the East Bank economy is able to sustain a larger trading deficit than would be the case if those dinars were used for purchases outside the West Bank, or were exchanged for foreign currencies. However, some dinars are exchanged for Israeli pounds and are a very useful source of hard currency for Israel. Also, in this sort of situation there is always the contingency that the economic or political situation might change so that the dinars might create a claim on the Jordanian reserves, which would no doubt force the Jordanian monetary authorities to place severe restrictions on convertibility.

INVESTMENT FUNDS

In the earlier sections of this chapter, the financial flows which have been discussed have been those associated with trade, public finance, and the holding of cash balances. Over the long term in the relations between developed and less-developed regions, however, the most strategic financial links are likely to be those involving private, direct investment, which create ownership links generating patterns of external economic control. While one should remain aware of the potential importance of such developments for the West Bank and the Gaza Strip, there is little evidence that Israeli investment has yet even begun to acquire such importance.

Both public and private investment in the West Bank and the Gaza Strip remained low for most of the period from 1967, picking up in 1972-73, and expanding considerably in the West Bank in 1974. The expansion in investment, when it came, was mainly through an increase in local private investment in vehicles and in buildings.

Total gross investment rose in 1972-73 to a level at which it accounted for 14 percent of the total resources used in the West Bank and the Gaza Strip—the total resources being defined as gross disposable private income (GDP) plus import surplus. In the preceding years it has been lower both absolutely and as a ratio to GDP. The public sector has provided a declining proportion of total investment, falling to only 21 percent of gross investment in 1972-73.

The available data are only suggestive. (See Table V-2). Growth in private investment apparently has been funded by the growth in private savings. Indeed, the level of private savings is now well in excess of private investment. An estimate of private savings—calculated as a residual after deducting estimated consumption from disposable income—indicates that from 1970 savings rose sharply. On the other hand, private investment did not rise significantly until 1972. Even with the sharp increase in investment in 1972, investment levels remained modest, and private savings continued in excess of private investment. These patterns all confirmed the likelihood of considerable hoarding, probably of dinars; and they further pointed to the existence of investment by residents of the West Bank in the East Bank economy. Too, the excess of savings over investment reflected a lack of local investment opportunities or uncertainty about the future. But a lag may have been involved; persistent high levels of savings could stimulate an active search for new investment outlets in the West Bank and the Gaza Strip. Data published more recently than that included in Table V-2 indicates that this has happened, in the West

Table V-2

Savings and Investment
(In Millions of Israeli Pounds at Current Prices)

	1968	1969	1970	1971	1972	1973
Gross disposable private income from all sources						
The West Bank	400	493	570	776	1,161	1,368
The Gaza Strip and North Sinai	167	198	262	352	539	789
Total	567	691	832	1,128	1,700	2,157
Private consumption expenditure						
The West Bank	359	452	496	635	908	1,144
The Gaza Strip and North Sinai	142	174	205	270	405	547
Total	501	626	701	905	1,313	1,691
Imputed private savings						
The West Bank	41	41	74	141	253	224
The Gaza Strip and North Sinai	25	24	57	82	134	242
Total	66	65	131	223	387	466

Bank at least. In 1974 there was a sharp increase in private investment activity there, particularly in building and construction. As a result, gross domestic capital formation in the West Bank doubled between 1973 and 1974.[10] But, there was no evidence in 1974 of any similar investment expansion in the Gaza Strip.

With relatively minor exceptions, Israeli private investors have not committed resources within the West Bank and the Gaza Strip outside those areas where new Israeli population settlements and industrial parks have been established since 1967. Conspicuous private Israeli investment in the territories for purposes not associated with Israeli settlements is primarily in the industrial estate on the border of the Gaza Strip, which utilizes Palestinian labor.[11] While this absence of private investment underlines the

	1968	1969	1970	1971	1972	1973
Gross domestic fixed capital formation from all sources						
The West Bank	25	51	62	87	145	198
The Gaza Strip and North Sinai	11	24	26	36	77	124
Total	36	75	88	123	222	322
Government and local authorities						
The West Bank	14	20	20	20	25	30
The Gaza Strip and North Sinai	4	15	16	19	28	38
Total	18	35	36	39	53	68
Private						
The West Bank	11	31	42	67	120	168
The Gaza Strip and North Sinai	7	9	10	17	49	86
Total	18	40	52	84	169	254

SOURCE: *Quarterly Statistics of the Administered Territories* (Jerusalem: Central Bureau of Statistics, 1974), Vol. IV, Nos. 3-4, pp. 77-85.

NOTE: Private savings is derived in this table as the residual after deducting private expenditure from disposable income.

specialized labor-supplying role of the territories, it has also meant, however, that within the two territories local businessmen have maintained a greater degree of autonomy than if there had been full-scale Israeli direct investment. Palestinian businesses are able to maintain independent trading or manufacturing activity for the local market or in subcontracting from Israeli firms, being subject neither to the prospect of takeover by Israeli firms nor to the local direct competition of Israeli firms setting up businesses in the local areas.

Although alternative patterns of investment involving the more complete economic integration of the West Bank and the Gaza Strip with Israel have been advocated by some leading Israeli figures, private investors have been unwilling to make permanent financial commitments. Trade and subcontracting enable Israeli businessmen to take advantage of immediate economic possibilities without becoming hostages to political fortune. This investment picture further confirms that, despite the degree of contact through trade and the labor market, there is a remarkable lack of integration of the financial and monetary systems.

As in the field of policies toward the use of Palestinian labor from the territories, in investment policy the Israeli authorities are faced with an awkward dilemma. If they encourage Israeli investment it would be seen as evidence of intent to annex the West Bank and the Gaza Strip economically and to occupy the territories indefinitely—one of the arguments that since 1967 has been leveled by Israeli critics themselves against more ambitious investment policies. Indeed, large-scale private Israeli investment would be most unlikely unless investors felt they enjoyed some long-term security. On the other hand, in the absence of industrial investment, the lop-sided character of the economies will continue and will reinforce the criticism that they are little more than dormitory areas for labor to support Israel's economy. This point is strengthened by the analysis in the next chapter, which indicates that labor earnings cannot continue to be the same stimulus to income growth as in the past.

THE IMPACT OF INFLATION

As a consequence of being attached to the Israeli economy, the West Bank and the Gaza Strip have become highly susceptible to the influence of general economic conditions in Israel, particularly the inflation. Repeated bouts of inflation resulted by the end of 1973 in an Israeli consumer price index roughly ten times its level in 1948. Between 1950 and 1973 the dollar value of the Israeli pound on the free market declined more than six-fold. Prices were relatively stable between 1967 and 1969 when upwards movements were of the order of 1 to 3 percent per annum, making this one of the most stable periods of Israeli price history. Subsequently, inflation accelerated so that by 1973 Israeli prices were rising at 20 percent per annum. This rate accelerated dramatically in 1974 and was given a further boost by the devaluation of November, 1974, and by subsequent devaluations. The period since 1973 has been one of worldwide inflation, but the Israeli experience was particularly severe.

Consumer price indices for the two territories after 1969 rose faster than in Israel. This was particularly evident in the Gaza Strip. One cause of this was that with the attraction of labor into Israel, wages were rising faster in both territories than they were in Israel, with the growth rate higher in Gaza.

Thus, even before the devaluation of the Israeli pound in November, 1974, the rate of price increase in the territories had been alarming (see Table V-3). By October, 1974, the consumer price index (Base: 100, July 1968-June 1969) had risen to 255.4 for the West Bank and 286.7 for the Gaza Strip. In November it jumped to 305.7 (West Bank) and 395.3 (Gaza)[12] and by March, 1975, had reached 363.1 (West Bank) and 444.8 (Gaza). Particularly because this dramatic inflation is in sharp contrast to the relative stability of the Jordanian price level, it is not surprising that it should be a source of local concern.

Inflation is always a matter of general inconvenience and there will always be some economic groups who suffer as a result. However, at least until 1974, inflation in the West Bank and the Gaza Strip was associated with the high rates of growth in real income and product. For the groups who participated in this income growth, inflation did not involve any loss of real income.

The lack of detailed income data means that it is not possible to specify which groups did lose as the result of inflation. Some of those who were already in employment at the beginning of the period of inflation will have suffered erosion in real income, but West Bank residents holding financial assets in dinars rather than Israeli pounds would not have suffered the losses sustained by Israelis who held Israeli currency. Detailed consumer price series, for various groups of commodities, do not suggest any pattern or systematic balance of advantage between differing economic groups.

The most recent data on output and employment for the period to the end of 1975 is not yet available. Vigorous inflation continues but the growth in real output may have been checked as a result of the dampening in Israeli economic activity. For the Palestinians of the West Bank and the Gaza Strip, this would mean that the problems arising from inflation are much greater, with a broader social group suffering.

In summary, while it is difficult to provide a fully elaborated account of the financial system of the West Bank and the Gaza Strip, the degree of autonomy of the Israeli banking system which has been maintained suggests a certain resilience of the local economy—there is a commercial and financial world within the

Table V-3

Consumer Price Index
(Excluding Housing)
(Base: July 1968-June 1969 = 100.0)

		The West Bank	The Gaza Strip
Average	1971	125.9	128.1
Average	1972	148.1	153.1
Average	1973	179.9	190.3
	January 1973	159.1	167.0
	February	162.7	166.2
	March	179.1	188.2
	April	178.2	195.3
	May	172.4	180.4
	June	170.3	180.8
	July	175.3	180.1
	August	178.5	186.8
	September	184.4	198.5
	October	190.1	205.3
	November	201.5	216.7
	December	207.1	218.7
	January 1974	226.4	235.4
	February	241.1	264.3
	March	245.5	268.7
	April	249.7	278.6
	May	240.5	277.4
	June	240.9	265.9
	July	243.1	270.7
	August	245.5	274.2
	September	251.9	287.2
	October	255.4	286.7
	November	305.7	395.3
	December	—	—

SOURCE: *Quarterly Statistics of the Administered Territories*, Vol. IV, Nos. 3-4, pp. 22-28.

Palestinian economy which is not incorporated into the picture painted from official statistics.

Footnotes

1. From 1968-69 to 1972-73 average public consumption fell from 14 percent to 10 percent of GNP. The decline as a percentage of gross do-

mestic product was somewhat less. GDP does not include wage earnings by residents in Israel.

2. For example, in an April, 1969, speech General Gazit, at that time Israeli military governor of the West Bank, said: "We must run the territories as cheaply as possible—and I am not only talking about money, though money is the first consideration." Quoted in Bernard Reich, "Israel and the Occupied Territories" (Washington, D.C.: Unpublished Paper Prepared for the Department of State External Research Program, August 1973), p. 4.

3. Arie Bregman, *Economic Growth in the Administered Areas, 1968-1973* (Jerusalem: Bank of Israel Research Department, 1975), p. 75.

4. While the oil fields of the Sinai were still under Israeli control, revenues were large enough to have a radical influence in the total budget picture for all Israeli-held territories. Thus, Sinai oil generated public revenues of 263.8 million Israeli pounds in the period 1970-71, over three-fifths of the estimated deficit in the civil budgets of all occupied territories combined. For further information and discussion of this and related issues, see Reich, *op. cit.,* pp. 10-13.

5. Bregman, *op. cit.,* p. 75. He does not provide details of the calculations used to arrive at his estimates, but they include an estimate of the fiscal burden for Israel of subsidized Israeli commodities consumed in the West Bank and the Gaza Strip.

6. Shabtai Teveth, *The Cursed Blessing: The Story of Israel's Occupation of the West Bank* (London: Weidenfeld and Nicolson, 1969), p. 150.

7. Bregman, *op. cit.,* p. 95. Presumedly the author means national product.

8. Note that Bregman claims after the August, 1971, devaluation of the Israeli pound, Palestinians in the occupied territories were more willing to hold Israeli currency. (See Bregman, *op. cit.,* p. 95.) Whether this remains true in view of the current performance of the Israeli pound would be interesting to know.

9. One unfortunate side effect of this, from the point of view of research, is a paucity of data on what has happened to the monetary phenomenon in the West Bank and the Gaza Strip. For example, there is no way of telling how far moneychangers, or merchants, who operate on a substantial scale and are sophisticated in handling international transactions, provide an informal financial network replacing some of the functions of the commercial banks.

10. *Quarterly Statistics of the Administered Territories,* Vol. V, No. 4 (Jerusalem: Central Bureau of Statistics, 1975), p. 107.

11. There are also occasional reports of individual investments, sometimes jointly with Arab businessmen (*e.g.,* stone quarrying), but there is no evidence to indicate any considerable activity.

12. All price data are adapted from various issues of the *Quarterly Statistics of the Administered Territories.*

Chapter 6

The Overall Impact on the Economics of the West Bank and the Gaza Strip

The change in external economic connections since 1967 has had dramatic effects within the West Bank and the Gaza Strip. It is possible to define the broad relationship between the developments described in Chapters 3 to 5 and major discernible internal economic trends within each territory.

What impact have these developments had on the overall pace of growth? Economists now recognize that the rate of growth of national income is not always a reliable indicator of economic progress, and needs to be evaluated alongside other, more qualitative, characteristics of the growth performance. However, "the growth rate" is still taken as the quickest and most straightforward measure of overall performance. Typically, Israeli spokesmen attach much positive significance to the high rates of economic growth achieved in the West Bank and the Gaza Strip since 1967. Particular attention is focused not only on the increase in incomes resulting from the growth of employment in Israel, but also on positive developments within the local economies, particularly in agriculture where highly beneficial transformations are attributed to the availability of Israeli technological assistance and advice.

Analysis of the overall growth performance particularly in terms of national income and agricultural output is, therefore, an essential part of any economic interpretation of the West Bank and Gaza Strip experience in recent years. While such an analysis may well be useful indirectly for political assessments, growth performance in itself, good or bad, will tell us nothing about the political acceptability of the existing situation in principle or about underlying political stability. Economic stagnation elsewhere in the world has been associated with political stability as well as with discontent, while economic growth has been associated with pressures for social change as well as with acceptance of the *status quo*.

OVERALL ECONOMIC GROWTH

There can be no doubt that the growth rate of the West Bank and the Gaza Strip has been high. Judgments may differ about the precise figures that should be used to describe the growth performance, but in absolute terms, and compared to previous experience here and with other economies, the growth has been impressive. The expansion of gross national product in the West Bank and Gaza Strip for 1968-1973 is set out in Table VI-1.

The Bank of Israel estimates real growth of the gross national product (*i.e.*, product including the incomes earned by Palestinians working in the Israeli economy) to have averaged 18 percent per annum, and per capita product to have grown at 15 percent per annum for 1968 to 1973. By international standards the Jordanian economy, including the West Bank, had already achieved a high rate of growth before 1967—8 percent per annum or higher—but there is no reason to suppose that growth rates anything like 18 percent were achieved.

Table VI-2 gives evidence of Jordan's growth before 1967, indicating a high growth performance, but also a high variability in growth from year to year, making growth trends over short periods difficult to assess.

The difficulty in assessing the significance of this West Bank and Gaza Strip growth since 1968 is two-fold.

First, the basic data are of uncertain reliability. As in any economy with substantial agricultural, handicraft and service activities, national income figures are difficult to put together and interpret, particularly in cases such as this when there has been a

Table VI-1 (1 of 3)

Gross National Product at Factor Cost in the Territories, by Economic Branch

(In Millions of Israeli Pounds at Current Prices)

	The Gaza Strip and North Sinai					
	1968	1969	1970	1971	1972	1973
Agriculture, forestry and fishing (including subsidies)	36	41	54	79	115	139
Industry	4	6	11	14	21	30
Construction (building and public works)	4	9	10	13	27	46
Public and community services*	26	30	37	49	66	94
Transport, trade and other services (including ownership of dwellings)	58	61	67	53	74	111
Errors and omissions**				52	55	96
Gross Domestic Product	128	147	179	260	358	516
Factor payments from abroad	2	9	30	46	129	226
Minus factor payments to abroad	2	2	3	4	5	6
Gross National Product (At factor cost)	128	154	206	302	482	736

(Table continued on page 118)

---

*Includes electricity and water services of the local authorities.

**Included to account for discrepancy between two alternative methods of estimating gross domestic product: according to value-added by industry of origin and according to use of resources.

SOURCE: Adapted from *Quarterly Statistics of the Administered Territories* (Jerusalem: Central Bureau of Statistics, 1974), Table 8,Vol. IV, Nos. 3-4, p. 84.

marked shift from peasant, semi-subsistence agriculture to wage employment.[1] Judicious interpretation of results is usually prudent for such cases, and undue precision should not be claimed. Nevertheless, the rates of growth for the West Bank and the Gaza Strip are high enough that even after very conservative downward

Table VI-1 (2 of 3)

Gross National Product at Factor Cost in the Territories, by Economic Branch

(In Millions of Israeli Pounds at Current Prices)

	The West Bank					
	1968	1969	1970	1971	1972	1973
Agriculture, forestry and fishing (including subsidies)	115	153	141	205	317	342
Industry	26	33	38	51	67	85
Construction (building and public works)	11	19	22	33	56	78
Public and community services*	56	60	67	84	109	139
Transport, trade and other services (including ownership of dwellings)	111	113	133	135	182	245
Errors and omissions**				31	87	60
Gross Domestic Product	319	378	401	539	818	949
Factor payments from abroad	17	50	89	175	296	373
Minus factor payments to abroad	6	8	9	11	12	15
Gross National Product (At factor cost)	330	420	481	703	1102	1307

(Table continued on page 119)

adjustments, the performance of these economies has been undeniably vigorous. Under normal circumstances, a growth rate of 3 to 4 percent per capita would be considered highly successful in a less-developed economy; 7 percent per capita performance would be quickly promoted into the "economic miracle" class.

Second, and perhaps more important, there is reason to doubt whether the estimates of output in the period immediately following the 1967 war are a meaningful baseline from which subsequent real growth ought to be measured. Because discussion of this problem is complex and in the end inconclusive, it has been banished to Appendix I, which discusses alternative approaches to estimating post-1968 growth in the two territories. In principle, it would be interesting to separate that element of observed growth which represents recovery from the disruption caused by war and

Table VI-1 (3 of 3)

**Gross National Product at Factor Cost in the
Territories, by Economic Branch**

(In Millions of Israeli Pounds at Current Prices)

	Total					
	1968	1969	1970	1971	1972	1973
Agriculture, forestry and fishing (including subsidies)	151	194	195	284	432	481
Industry	30	39	49	65	88	115
Construction (building and public works)	15	28	32	46	83	124
Public and community services*	82	90	104	133	175	233
Transport, trade and other services (including ownership of dwellings)	169	174	200	188	256	356
Errors and omissions**				83	142	156
Gross Domestic Product	447	525	580	799	1176	1465
Factor payments from abroad	19	59	119	221	425	599
Minus factor payments to abroad	8	10	12	15	17	21
Gross National Product (At factor cost)	458	574	687	1005	1584	2043

occupation, from that part which is an expansion to levels of income and output above the pre-1967 level. But these two components of subsequent growth are not readily distinguishable for several reasons: the pre-1967 data are very limited; there was a substantial decline in population in 1967-68; there was a change in geographical coverage because of the exclusion of Jerusalem from West Bank data after 1967; and there were substantial increases in prices.

Despite these difficulties, the implications of conservative, yet plausible adjustments, are clear enough in outline: As the detailed rationale in the appendix suggests, a conservative estimate of the growth rate from 1968-1973, over and above postwar recovery, can be estimated at about 9 percent per annum or between 6 and 7 percent per capita.

Table VI-2

Jordan:
Gross National Product, 1960-67
(In Constant 1967 Prices)

	1960	1961	1962	1963	1964	1965	1966	1967
Gross national product (in millions of dollars)	296	356	366	385	450	506	520	575
Percent of change from previous year		20.3	2.8	5.2	16.9	12.4	2.8	10.6
Per capita gross national product (in dollars)	179	210	210	214	244	267	266	286
Percent of change in per capita gross national product from previous year		17.3	0	1.9	14.2	9.4	—0.4	7.5

NOTE: Jordanian national income accounts are not corrected for price changes.

SOURCE: Adapted from Eliyahu Kanovsky, *The Economic Impact of the Six-Day War* (New York: Praeger, 1970), Table 21, p. 437.

The Effect of Employment in Israel

This growth performance can be interpreted and partially explained in the light of the various economic factors discussed in the other sections of this study.

In particular, it is interesting to estimate the impact of employment in Israel; Table VI-1 indicates quite dramatically how important is the estimated growth in income earned outside the territories—almost all from employment in Israel—as a factor in total growth.

In effect, *over one-third* of the increase in gross national product is accounted for directly by the increase in wage earnings in Israel. It should be noted, however, that this exogenous injection of income into the territories also has indirect effects on the level of economic activity. There are two ways of viewing these indirect effects.

From the point of view of *aggregate demand* the injection of the additional income provided by these wage earnings fuels a multiplier process, whereby the expenditures of wage earners generate additional income flows. This stimulus could be viewed as a major influence on the level of economic activity within the territories.

Alternatively, in most less-developed economies the immediate constraint on the level of expenditure is the *supply constraint* created by the limited availability of foreign exchange. Such an argument cannot be applied straightforwardly to this case, because, as we have seen, the West Bank and the Gaza Strip have neither their own currency nor an autonomous fiscal policy. There is therefore no possibility for public authorities to push the economy to the limits of a potential foreign exchange constraint. As a stimulus to aggregate demand, then, the expenditure multiplier effect in this instance is limited because:

(1) Imports of goods and services are a very high ratio of GNP. In 1973, these imports totaled 1,167 million Israeli pounds, or 57 percent of GNP, at factor cost. This means that a large part of the initial impact of the increase in spending resulting from the rise in wage earnings would flow directly into imports, primarily from Israel.

(2) A part of the increase in income will have substituted for income which would otherwise have been generated in the territories, insofar as the transfer in labor resulted in a drop in production in some sectors in the territories.

(3) Evidence on savings propensities suggests, as indicated in Chapter 5, that private savings have been significant and have tended to result in the accumulation of the monetary balances or in investment outside the territories, as much as in local investment, at least until 1973. The expansion of investment in the West Bank during 1974 might change this picture by suggesting that eventually the growth in employment incomes does stimulate investment activity. No account is taken of that in this calculation.

Appendix I, after calculating savings and import propensities from available aggregate statistics, suggests a multiplier for foreign earnings of 1.5. If some proportion of employment income outside the West Bank and the Gaza Strip is at the expense of production within the territories, the multiplier must be reduced accordingly. An educated guess would be that such substitution would unlikely be more than 20 percent of these outside employment incomes. This suggests a multiplier in the range of 1.2 to 1.5. If the growth in these incomes itself generates additional incomes through acceleration in investment activity, then the effect will be accordingly greater.

From Table VI-3 we note that net factor incomes from abroad accounted for 35 percent of the growth in GNP in 1968-1973. If the full multiplier effect of 1.5 had taken effect, then 53 percent of the growth in GNP could be traced directly or indirectly to the growth in incomes earned outside the West Bank and the Gaza Strip. If the substitution element was 20 percent this income source would still account for as much as 42 percent of GNP growth.

The conclusion that the contribution of employment earnings outside the territories was somewhere around one-half of the total growth seems reasonable. This was the major stimulating factor distinguishing the post-1967 economy from the pre-war situation. Applying this rough estimate to the growth rates achieved, one concludes that the estimated growth not explained by this factor[2] would be 8.5 to 10.5 percent per annum. Given the likelihood discussed above that 1968 represents a base year which had not yet achieved post-war recovery, then the 8.5 to 10.5 percent growth rate is not out of line with either estimates of growth in Jordan before 1967 or those in the East Bank in recent years.

One important implicaton of this arithmetic, rough as it is, needs to be emphasized. Given the proportion of the active work force of the territories now employed in Israel, even if the Israeli economy were to sustain another boom, there is little likelihood of employment growth in residents of the territories in Israel playing the same role *as a source of growth* in the territories as it did in the period 1968-1973. Another arithmetic speculation will demonstrate the point. If the West Bank and Gaza Strip economies were to grow at 15 percent per annum in real terms, 1973-1978, so that GNP doubles, and "net earnings from abroad" were to account for half that growth, they would have to expand from 578 million Israeli pounds to 1259 million Israeli pounds (1973 prices) to make the same proportionate contributions to growth as in the 1968-1973 period. That is, they would need to grow over that period 17 percent per annum.[3] Even making generous estimates of growth in real wages in Israel (say 5 to 7 percent per annum), this would require a continuing growth of 10 to 12 percent in the level of employment of Palestinians from the territories in Israel, suggesting an increase in jobs of 40,000 to 50,000 over the levels already reached. While not an impossible figure, it seems extremely unlikely. It would involve a high degree of acceptance of Palestinian labor in an increasing range of activities in Israel, the employment of nearly 50 percent of the

Table VI-3

Contribution of Earnings from Abroad to Growth: 1968-1973

(In Millions of Israeli Pounds)

	1968	1973	Growth 1968-73
The West Bank			
Gross national product	330	1307	977
Net factor payment from abroad	11	358	347
Net factor payment from abroad as percent of GNP	3.3	27.4	35.5
The Gaza Strip			
Gross national product	128	736	608
Net factor payment from abroad		220	220
Net factor payment from abroad as percent of GNP		29.9	36.2
Total			
Gross national product	458	2043	1585
Net factor payment from abroad	11	578	567
Net factor payment from abroad as percent of GNP	2.4	28.3	35.8

Palestinian labor force in the Israeli economy and a renewed boom in the Israeli economy. However, as that proportion increases so does the likelihood that the withdrawal of Palestinian labor from the territories will reduce the level of economic activity there. The net impact will therefore be reduced, so that even the suggested magnitude of growth in employment would not make the necessary contribution to the rate of growth in GNP.

EFFECTS ON THE ECONOMIC STRUCTURE

The Industrial Sector

Industrial activity in the West Bank and the Gaza Strip was modest in 1968 and has remained modest. As Table VI-1 indicates, industry accounted for only 7 percent of gross domestic product in 1968. By 1973 this had only risen to 8 percent. As a percentage of gross national product, industrial activity declined from 7 percent to 6 percent. The number employed in industry expanded from 18,000 in 1968 to 20,000 in 1973, but was still only 15 percent of total employment in the two territories. The fact that industry continues to account for a higher proportion of employment than output deserves comment, for it seems to conflict with the usual economic pattern, in which the manufacturing industry tends to be the highest productivity sector. In this case, part of the explanation is that a significant segment of gross domestic product is generated in the agricultural sector, where much of the work is done by family labor that does not enter the employment statistics. Also, much of the so-called industrial activity in the West Bank and the Gaza Strip is craftwork in low-productivity, labor-intensive activities.

The detailed composition of industrial activity is no more than that typical of the least industrialized primary exporting nations, the largest activities being the food, beverage and tobacco industry and the olive oil presses—activities closely associated with processing agricultural products for local and export use.

The only indication of any change in industrial structure is the accelerated development of some activities producing for the Israeli market—particularly building materials and subcontracting activities, especially clothing. Clothing manufacture has grown at a very high rate, at over 30 percent per annum from 1969 to 1972 in both territories.[4] While it has become a significant part of the small industrial sector of the Gaza Strip, accounting for 23 percent of sales in 1972, it is still a very minor part of the West Bank economy. The high growth rate started from such a small base that total impact is still small. And, as the clothing industry mainly utilizes low-paid female labor for the labor-intensive steps in the manufacture of clothing, the financial contribution to the economies of the West Bank and the Gaza Strip is much smaller than the gross flow of trade in clothing would suggest.

As indicated in Chapter 4, one should be cautious about assigning great importance to the impact of subcontracting. Nevertheless, if the existing economic relations are maintained, what has happened so far could prove to be the early beginnings of a more important trend. The subcontracting system is entirely based on the availability of cheap labor. The growth of the system will require an increasing mobilization of female labor, since the alternative employment opportunities make it unlikely that there will be a ready supply of low-wage male industrial labor. It can be argued that subcontracting-related employment provides jobs for the workers who are unlikely to find incomes elsewhere. It can also be argued, however, that it only survives as long as wages are low, and that, because it involves only the labor-intensive steps in industrial processes originating and being completed in Israel, its contributions to the industrial development of the territories will be minimal.

Apart from the subcontracting phenomenon, the most notable characteristic of the industrial situation in the West Bank and the Gaza Strip is the *absence* of substantial new industrial development. In the absence of protection specifically directed to the needs of industry in the territories and of other public measures to promote industry, and with the insecurity about the long-term future inherent in the political situation, the lack of new industrial initiatives is not surprising. As stressed earlier, there is no easy industrialization strategy here. The local market is small, so that few industries could be efficiently based on import substitution. But given the limited raw material base of the territories, industrial development is just as necessary for their development as it has been for Israel. A policy of changing the economic structure to provide an effective base for industry was followed neither by Jordan before 1967, nor by Israel since; it is a long-term project which has yet to begin.

The Service Sector

Services include a multifarious range of activities, such as transport, trade and finance, hotels, government services, etc. There are few generalizations to be made about such a wide range of activities, or the impact of the external economic changes on them. However, there have been some noteworthy effects on specific segments.

Tourism had been an important source of income before 1967, particularly in the West Bank. Since 1967 the limitations on Arab tourists who made up more than half the pre-1966 visitors and the shift in Christian tourists towards utilization of Israeli facilities as a base for their visits to the religious sites have undermined the once-thriving tourist industry. Jordan had attracted almost twice as many tourists as Israel in 1966 and income from tourism accounted for about 30 percent of Jordan's current account export earnings. It has been estimated that the tourist income of the West Bank was 6 to 7 million Jordanian dinars in 1966, of which 5 to 6 million was spent in Jerusalem.[5] Including the 1 million dinars earned from East Bank tourists, the earnings from tourism equaled about one-third of total imports of goods from the East Bank and abroad.

Since the annexation of East Jerusalem, the main center of tourist spending has tended to shift to the Israeli hotels.[6] The decline in tourist trade throughout the rest of the West Bank is partly indicated by the decline in the average rate of hotel occupancy from about 50 percent before 1967 to 15 percent in 1969, rising to 37 percent in 1972 and falling back to 31 percent in 1973.[7] At the same time hotel capacity has stagnated since 1970.

The setback for the tourist industry has been one of the most important negative consequences for the West Bank of the situation since 1967. Particularly as incomes have expanded so rapidly in the oil-producing Arab states, there is a potential market for rapid expansion; instead the industry has gone into decline.

Transport System. Also important has been the reorientation of the transport system. The basic lines of communication from the West Bank to the outside world now pass through Israel, which provides a more direct trading route.

The Gaza port has remained well below its full potential. Following 1967, the Gaza Strip gained access to the West Bank and to Jordan, resulting in some trade in agricultural products. As was noted in Chapter 1, in the pre-1948 era Gaza had provided port facilities for parts of southern Palestine—indeed, Gaza is closer to Amman than are the two major ports serving Jordan—Aqaba, in Jordan, or Beirut. Gaza currently has a capacity of 250,000 tons a year as an open seaport where ships are served by lighters from jetties. With an active policy and supporting measures it could easily be expanded to handle three to four times that trade as a commercial center or as an entrepôt for the West Bank.

Financial and Commercial Services. Likewise striking, in relation to financial services, is the absence of a full-scale commercial banking system. There nevertheless is a web of small and medium-scale financial and commercial ventures that do make up a system of finance not described in available published sources, and it is therefore difficult to assess the past or future role of such businesses.

It is clear that one important question is how far Jerusalem has continued to play a focal financial and commercial role in the existing pattern of relationships. Before 1967, East Jerusalem was the biggest town on the West Bank and the largest commercial center, and its role as a tourist center alone would have given Jerusalem extraordinary economic prominence. The development of

Amman as the major administrative and commercial center of Jordan from 1948 to 1967 shifted the focus of economic life in Jordan towards the East Bank and meant that Jerusalem was not a great metropolitan pole of growth. Nevertheless, it provided the largest market on the West Bank, had the best developed services and, in addition, was the natural connection for transport between the northern and southern parts of the West Bank. Thus, while Jerusalem was less than a *de facto* commercial and administrative capital of the West Bank, it was the most important center of economic activity. Even with the fiscal and juridical integration of East Jerusalem into Israel, economic connections have persisted between the city's Arab community and the rest of the West Bank.

The Agricultural Sector

As might be expected for an economy at this stage of development, the most important domestic activity in the two territories is agriculture. In 1968, 35 percent of employed persons were directly involved in the agricultural sector. As we have seen, the major part of the commodity export trade from the territories to Jordan and overseas is derived from agricultural output.

The effects of the changing external circumstances of the West Bank and the Gaza Strip on the agricultural sector since 1968 are not clear-cut. Fundamental changes in agricultural systems take many years for their full effects to become discernible. The data for 1968-73 are likely to reflect mainly changes resulting from the short-term fluctuations typical in agriculture, especially agriculture in the West Bank which is largely dependent on rain because of a very limited development of irrigation. Also, data are not sufficient to identify the detailed effects of changing markets.

The most important likely impact in the agricultural sector of the changing external economic relations has been outlined in the earlier discussion of trade and employment. To summarize:

(1) Trading patterns changed with the emergence of a market for agricultural products from the territories in Israel itself, the competition from the products of Israeli agriculture, and the practice of exporting to markets abroad through the agency of Israeli intermediaries.

(2) Employment declined in the agricultural sector as job opportunities expanded in the Israeli economy.

(3) Agriculture gained access to Israeli advice and technology.

Initially after the 1967 war, when Israeli authorities were concerned that agricultural surpluses from the territories would enter Israel and upset the markets for Israeli agriculture, every effort was made to continue pre-war trade patterns. The West Bank continued to export to Jordan, and the overseas contracts of the Gaza Strip citrus industry were fulfilled. By 1970-71, however, the restrictions on exports from the territories to Israel were reduced and a process of partial integration of agriculture sectors was set in motion.

Israel has made some effort to adjust the pattern of agricultural production in the territories so that it complements rather than competes with the Israeli pattern. But in general, the agricultural sectors of the West Bank and the Gaza Strip are predominantly competitive with Israeli production. The agricultural sector of the territories has had to compete with Israeli agricultural products that are in some cases subsidized by the government. Table VI-4 gives a picture of the changing pattern of agricultural activity on the West Bank. Most notable was the shift away from melons towards production of vegetables and tree crops. The reduction of the area under cultivation, particularly the area utilized for field crops, reflects the sharp drop in agricultural employment in the West Bank demonstrated in Table VI-5. Similarly the shift in the pattern of land use in part reflects this reduction in labor input; the planting of orchards involves a shift to agricultural systems less labor-intensive than production of field crops. The expansion of the area under irrigation represents an improvement in technology involving better use of existing water supplies, rather than substantial development of new basic sources of water.

It is difficult to interpret the available output figures. The largest single crop is olives, utilizing more than half a million dunams of land. It takes some years for an olive tree to come into production; production in the period we are examining will be from trees planted before 1967. Moreover, the output of olives from the West Bank has always been highly volatile. For example, before 1967 the output of olives in Jordan, the major part of which came from the West Bank, varied from 114,000 metric tons in 1961 to 7,000 in 1962, 39,000 in 1963, up to 98,000 in 1964. The record for the period since 1967, as set out in Table VI-6, indicates that the largest single element in year-to-year changes in agricultural output has resulted from changes in the olive crop, rising from 15,000 tons in the 1969-70 season to 70,000 tons in 1971-72.

Table VI-4

The West Bank: Land Use
in Agriculture
(In Thousands of Dunams*)

	1968	1973
Total Cultivated Area	2045	2017**
Field crops	890	827
wheat	465	430
barley	231	150
vetch	48	30
sesame	18	40
lentils	61	60
chick peas	32.5	80
tobacco	4.5	6
others	30	31
Orchards	680	765
olives	514	580
grapes	54	62
citrus fruits	24	24
figs	38	15
almonds	34	61
others	17	23
Melons	43	10
Vegetables	70	80
In preparation	362	335
Included in the above:		
Irrigated Area	57	81
Vegetables	31	54
Citrus fruits	24	24.5
Bananas	2	2.5

* A dunam is approximately one-quarter of an acre.

** In the original source this total was shown as 2022;
however, the correct sum of the sub-totals is 2017
as shown here. It is not possible to identify the
source of the error from published data.

SOURCE: *West Bank Agriculture 1973* (Ramallah:
Agricultural Department of the West Bank,
No. 147, August 1974), pp. 6-8.

Table VI-5

The West Bank: Agricultural Inputs

People Employed in Agriculture

Year	Total employed	Hired laborers
1970	45,000	11,200
1971	39,900	10,000
1972	38,500	9,800
1973	33,500	7,500

Use of Inputs

	1968	1970	1972	1973	1974
Use of fertilizers (in thousands of tons)	4,000	6,800	8,000	11,000	
Number of tractors	120	455	740	866	1,100

SOURCE: *West Bank Agriculture 1973*, p. 9.

This expansion is not necessarily an indication, however, of any underlying growth in productivity. The levels achieved in 1971-72 are quite in line with the peak levels before 1967, particularly as in 1966 young orchards of olives accounted for some 20 percent of the acreage already in production.

While those products benefiting from both a market opportunity in Israel and an improvement in production techniques as a result of access to Israeli technology have expanded, growth in total agricultural output has not been substantial. Indeed, compared with peak years prior to 1967, it seems doubtful whether total output has expanded at all. Table IV-4 (Chapter 4, p. 92) gives some indication, however, of the agricultural export trade. In relation to the commodities covered—that is, fruits and vegetables—just over one-third of a local production of 510,000 tons was exported. The largest export market was still Jordan. The Israeli and overseas market accounted for only some 12 percent of local production, the larger part of this being vegetable sales. On the other hand the decline in production of melons and pumpkins in the West Bank has been associated with an increase in imports of these items from Israel. Interestingly, the West Bank has become a net importer of fruits and vegetables—especially citrus fruits—from the Gaza Strip.

Many commentaries on agriculture in the territories in 1967 emphasize the very low level of technique and frequently criticize

Table VI-6 (1 of 2 tables)

Growth in Agricultural Output

	The West Bank		
	1967/68	1971/72	1972/73
Value in Millions of Israeli Pounds			
Total Output	135.0	347.1	399.5
Crops	87.9	233.3	253.9
field crops	11.0	37.2	48.7
vegetables	19.5	54.4	60.9
melons and pumpkins	6.0	1.5	1.5
olives	19.6	73.5	52.5
citrus fruits	10.5	18.1	27.1
other fruits	21.3	48.6	63.2
Livestock and livestock products	45.0	110.5	142.5
meat	25.1	70.1	90.2
milk	15.7	32.5	43.1
eggs	3.2	7.0	7.2
miscellaneous	1.0	1.9	2.0
fish	—	—	—
Investments in forestry and new fruit plantations	2.1	3.3	3.1
Purchased Inputs	21.4	42.9	63.5
Income Originating in Agriculture	113.6	307.1	336.0
Quantity in Thousands of Tons			
Field crops	23.5	55.3	43.3
Vegetables	60.0	103.1	93.4
Melons and pumpkins	36.0	8.0	3.3
Olives	28.0	70.0	21.0
Citrus fruits	30.0	47.6	58.6
Other fruits	47.9	56.5	58.9
Meat	10.3	18.7	20.9
Milk	30.3	43.8	44.3
Eggs (million)	25.0	30.0	38.0
Fish	—	—	—

SOURCE: *Statistical Abstract of Israel 1974*
(Jerusalem: Central Bureau of Statistics,
1974), Table xxvi/26, p. 708.

Table VI-6 (2 of 2 tables)

Growth in Agricultural Output

	The Gaza Strip and North Sinai		
	1967/68	1971/72	1972/73
Value in Millions of Israeli Pounds			
Total Output	53.3	149.5	192.2
Crops	41.3	113.8	140.9
field crops	0.3	1.3	1.7
vegetables	9.3	16.9	20.6
melons and pumpkins	2.5	2.5	3.4
olives	—	—	—
citrus fruits	21.6	75.6	92.0
other fruits	7.6*	17.5*	23.2
Livestock and livestock products	10.9	33.9	49.5
meat	3.6	12.7	17.3
milk	3.3	7.3	12.2
eggs	1.1	3.8	4.9
miscellaneous	0.2	0.3	0.5
fish	2.7	9.8	14.6
Investments in forestry and new fruit plantations	1.1	1.8	1.8
Purchased Inputs	17.0	42.1	61.8
Income Originating in Agriculture	36.3	105.5	128.9
Quantity in Thousands of Tons			
Field crops			
Vegetables	31.8	38.9	42.5
Melons and pumpkins	12.5	4.6	5.0
Olives	—	—	—
Citrus fruits	91.0	178.0	205.2
Other fruits	19.0*	26.3*	21.4*
Meat	1.7	3.0	3.5
Milk	6.8	9.7	11.2
Eggs (million)	10.0	24.0	30.0
Fish	3.7	4.2	4.6

* Including olives.

the high degree of labor-intensiveness. But it is important to recognize that, where labor is cheap and jobs outside agriculture are not available, the utilization of large amounts of labor in agriculture makes good economic sense. A judgment about the extent of technical transformation since 1967 is complicated. Some of the reduction in employment is associated with marginal land previously farmed by small farmers but withdrawn from production as these farmers turned their attention to the possibilities of wage employment in the Israeli labor market. Some part also represents a drop in disguised unemployment on family farms still in production.

Certain technological improvements, no doubt, have been important. But the use of plastic covers in vegetable production and a considerable improvement in irrigation techniques, however valuable in themselves, have affected a rather minor part of the total acreage involved in the agricultural sector. The purchase of inputs by farmers has expanded in line with the growth in farm sales. The continuing low level of input purchases suggests that there has been no dramatic qualitative transformation in farm technology.

There are no official Israeli data showing the value of farm outputs at fixed prices. A rough index can be made for the growth in real output in agriculture using the content as shown in Table VI-7, and valuing outputs at 1967-68 prices. This calculation suggests that total output had risen some 70 percent by 1971-72 over 1967-68 levels. But in 1972-73, which was not such a good year climatically, the level of output fell back, with an increase of only 45 percent over the 1967-68 level. Because output was very low in 1967-68 compared with previous years, little growth in output is implied by these figures.

Possibly one of the most striking things about agriculture in the territories as compared both with Israeli agriculture and, increasingly, with agriculture in Jordan, is the very limited development of irrigation. During the period of Jordanian rule most of the irrigation development was on the East Bank of the Jordan River. In addition most of the plans for future developments also involved projects located in the East Bank.

One consequence of depending primarily on rain-fed agricultural production is the high risks involved. An agricultural system operating under such uncertainty would not be in a position either to risk heavy investments in mechanization or to carry a high financial burden in the form of wage costs.

Table VI-7

Growth in Real Output of Agriculture: West Bank

Crops	Prices 1967/68 (Israeli pounds per ton)	1971/72 output (in millions of Israeli pounds at 1967/68 prices)	1972/73 output (in millions of Israeli pounds at 1967/68 prices)
Field Crops	468	25.9	20.3
Vegetables and Potatoes	325	33.5	30.4
Melons and Pumpkins	167	1.3	0.6
Olives	700	49.0	14.7
Citrus	350	16.7	20.5
Other Fruits	446	25.2	26.3
Livestock and Livestock Produce			
Meat	2437	45.6	50.9
Milk	518	22.7	22.9
Eggs (per 1,000)	128	3.8	4.9
Total		223.7	191.5

Output growth since 1967/68:
1971/72 output valued at 1967/68 prices as ratio of 1967/68 output value: 1.696

1972/73 output valued at 1967/68 prices as ratio of 1967/68 output value: 1.452

SOURCE: Adapted from data in Table VI-6.

The overall agricultural picture supports one central conclusion: The main impact of the contact with Israel since 1967 has been reduction in the level of employment in the agricultural sector, without large-scale changes in the structure and levels of output. Except for certain limited sectors, major changes have not occurred in techniques of production—both conclusions being somewhat more skeptical than those of some other commentators.[8]

If current trends continue, the impact on the agricultural sector is likely to be much more profound. As the wage rate increases in the territories and labor becomes more scarce, the agricultural sector will be faced with two alternative paths of development. If technical advice is available and if funds and the willingness to invest are there, the agricultural sector might go through a process of mechanization and increased expenditure on the purchase of inputs involving increases in the productivity per man and productivity per acre.

However, insofar as farmers are not willing to invest and are faced with competition from the output of Israeli agriculture, some of which is subsidized, the sector could be faced with dangerous stagnation. As the pull of employment opportunities drains the countryside of labor, if there is a failure to transform agricultural methods to operate under the new conditions, then the sector will shrink. The poor development of irrigation capacity in the territories is likely to become the increasingly critical factor. In the absence of an assured water supply, the risk of making other forms of capital investment seriously restrains the required impetus toward technical change in the sector.

These, then, are the principal legacies of the past nine years on the economic life of the West Bank and the Gaza Strip, as they can be ascertained from the aggregate data used in this discussion. While sector-by-sector microeconomic analysis would no doubt be more revealing, this overview captures the essentials of what has happened. The next, final chapter explores, more speculatively, some of the implications of these findings.

Footnotes

1. The difficulty with these data is indicated by the size of the "errors and omissions" items in the table showing gross domestic product by economic branch. These items are included to balance this series with the estimate of gross domestic product on the basis of resource-use. By 1973 errors and omissions were just over 10 percent of the gross domestic product.

2. Taking the real growth rate of 18 percent per annum, 1968-1973; this method jumps one step in the analysis as the discussion of the immediately preceding pages has been in terms of the observed growth of national product and foreign income in current prices, while the real growth rate is in *constant* prices. There is, therefore, an implicit assumption that if employment in Israel explains 40 percent of observed growth

in the level of spending in current prices, this will also represent 40 percent of real growth.

3. Assuming a multiplier of 1.5.

4. See Arie Bregman, *Economic Growth in the Administered Areas, 1968-1973* (Jerusalem: Bank of Israel Research Department, 1975), p. 64, Table IV-4. The author's use of the concept of output is not clearly defined in this instance.

5. Economic Planning Authority, *Economic Survey of the West Bank (Summary)* (Jerusalem: December, 1967), p. 19.

6. Haim Ben Shahar, E. Berglas, Y. Mundlak, and E. Sadan, *Economic Structure and Development Prospects of the West Bank and the Gaza Strip* (Santa Monica, California: The Rand Corporation, 1971), p. 122.

7. Bregman, *op. cit.,* p. 83; and *Statistical Abstract, 1974,* p. 714.

8. In comparison, Vivian Bull in *The West Bank—Is it Viable?* (Lexington, Massachusetts: D. C. Heath and Co., 1975), p. 89, concludes that "there has been impressive development within the agricultural sector since 1967." She suggests (pp. 71-89) that this development is a major and positive fact of the connection with Israel. On the other hand, Bregman is more cautious in his assessment, pointing out, correctly, some of the positive developments, but, overall, largely laying hope for future benefits to be derived from the Israeli connection rather than making claims for achievements not yet sustained. (See Bregman, *op. cit.,* pp. 48-54.)

Chapter 7

Economic Issues and the Future

This study was written in 1975 and early 1976, when the political future of the West Bank and the Gaza Strip became the object of greatly intensified interest both internationally and in the territories themselves. However, the political events sketched in the opening pages of the prologue were a clear reminder that, for all parties involved in the future of the territories, the cardinal questions do not turn on economic issues *per se.* Nevertheless, this study's review of crucial economic dimensions of Israeli rule over the West Bank and the Gaza Strip supports several observations.

- Cumulatively, the economic developments affecting the West Bank and the Gaza Strip since 1967 have introduced important new elements in the overall picture. The years since 1967 have witnessed the evolution of a new network of economic interests, a new pattern of economic interdependence, and a new mixture of economic benefits and burdens among the four economies—Israel, the West Bank, the Gaza Strip and Jordan. There is, in other words, a new economic *status quo,* a new set of expectations about what a continuation of that *status quo* implies, and a new mix of strong reactions welcoming or resisting those implications among the parties most directly concerned. In 1967, extensive discussion about the desirability of one or another political future for the two territories could have been carried on—and, indeed was carried on—without reference to the economic consequences of those contemplated changes. No longer is that possible—even though it remains true that economic factors do not decisively shape either the political preferences of the parties or their willingness to tolerate alternative political futures. From this a second observation follows.

- No significant change in the political status of the territories can now be seriously negotiated, or contemplated unilaterally by Israel, without attracting attention to its economic repercussions. Even perpetuation of the *status quo* has adverse social-economic implications not only for the territories but for Israel as well. At one extreme, were Israel to move toward annexation of the territories these implications would have to be faced. Or, at the other extreme, were the territories to move toward any degree of political autonomy or independence, resultant economic opportunities and constraints would enter the political calculations. Put simply, the perceived or real economic stakes, satisfactions, sources of leverage, and grievances now characterizing the economic situation did not exist in their present form in 1967. New considerations would be brought into play if responsible authorities in the four economies had to articulate and defend their economic self-interests vis-à-vis the others. There would be contending pressures and incentives: to maintain the network of economic relationships in essentially its present form, to change it marginally, or to reorient it radically. Preferences for one or another of these tendencies have already been voiced in the political programs of the interested parties. Viewed solely from the vantage point of the West Bank and the Gaza Strip, political autonomy or independence would create new scope to pursue economic self-interests. And the broader that scope, the broader the opportunities to accept, reject, or tailor the economic inheritance of the past nine years, and indeed of the past twenty-eight years.

- Just as economic interests have become increasingly a part of the new factual reality facing Israel, the West Bank and the Gaza Strip, and Jordan, so too have economic rationales crept increasingly into the political debate about what is possible or not, desirable or not, prudent or not, in any political future.

There is an intriguing range of perspectives on the economic contexts of differing political outcomes. To defend the Israeli acquisition of the West Bank in 1967, some analysts argued that Israel had not, as charged, destroyed Jordan's economic prospects by lopping off a most productive segment of the kingdom. To the contrary, the argument implied, Jordan might even be better off economically without the West Bank—which never had been integrated into Jordan anyway. To buttress claims after 1967 that the West Bank must remain economically tied to Israel, or re-attached to the Jordanian economy—but in either case not become independent—both pro-Israeli and pro-Jordanian viewpoints began from the premise that a separate West Bank or West Bank-Gaza Strip political unit would not be economically viable; Israeli as well as Jordanian spokesmen have said it often. Proponents of an independent entity, on the other hand, argue that economic viability is a result of economic policies and resources—not some static or fixed measure of inherent economic capabilities. Some pro-Palestinian proponents go farther. They argue not only that viability is possible via some "normal" economic relations with neighboring economies and the international economy beyond, but also that political dominance by Israel and Jordan can be avoided by an independent Palestinian entity composed of the West Bank and the Gaza Strip only *if* it is economically independent of *both* Israeli and Jordanian economies.

Some Palestinians arguing the case against the persistent pursuit of maximal objectives insist that one objection to the realization of a democratic secular state in all of historic Palestine would be that the Palestinian community within it would inevitably be overwhelmed by the economic superiority of the Jewish community; therefore, the argument runs, it would better suit the Palestinians to have a separate state of their own alongside Israel, at least until more competitive economic and technological capabilities can be built up. Still other Palestinians have taken for granted that a Palestinian state alongside Israel can be viable, but they argue further that such a state should not avoid economic interpenetration with the Israeli economy—it should welcome it under certain political conditions.

Segments of both Israeli and Palestinian opinion accept, though draw different conclusions from, the premise that any independent Palestinian entity would not be viable economically.

Palestinians who reject any political compromise that would give legitimacy to the idea of a West Bank-Gaza Strip ministate by asserting that it would be economically unviable, vulnerable to economic domination by more powerful Israeli and Jordanian neighbors, and therefore subject to a kind of stagnation that would permanently sidetrack the Palestinian cause. There are those Israeli critics of the ministate idea who would agree that the prospect of dominance by the superior neighboring economies is real, but they conclude that this very prospect would be one of the frustrations inevitably pushing such a political entity to relentless irredentism and hostility against one or both of its larger neighbors.

Nor, it may be added as a final illustration, are economic arguments marshaled only to support long-term visions. They are also involved in arguments about the short term. When Israeli Defense Minister Shimon Peres unveiled in late 1975 a new version of his long-favored plan to grant local self-administration to West Bank Palestinians, Israeli critics said the idea was incompatible with the essential premises of the occupation. Self-administered West Bank Palestinians, the critics argued, would immediately move to establish their own authority to a degree that would challenge Israel's control over transactions that generate revenues for the West Bank, such as collection of tariffs and taxes at the Jordan River bridges.

Economic arguments are not equally important to each of these lines of political analysis; nor are the economic assumptions equally well-founded in all cases. Some, obviously, are flimsy and simply self-serving. Indeed the variety and the manifest contradictions of many of these arguments tend to confirm that some economic arguments often are shaped less by economic realities than by historical, political, and ideological perceptions.

These general observations lead to three questions about the overall pattern of economic developments surveyed in this study, each of which will be addressed in the remainder of this chapter.

First: Which elements in this new picture of economic interconnections since 1967 are most important in their implications for the West Bank and the Gaza Strip? The heightened attention on the political future of these territories, the interplay of political interests with economic considerations, and the widely disparate political and analytic verdicts on the economic dimension of the nine years of Israeli rule—all suggest the value of a judgment about what is fundamental and what is secondary in the overall economic picture traced in this study.

Second: What economic self-interests flowing from these developments during the past nine years are likely to be seen—from the point of view of each of the involved economies—as important to pursue in the future, and how might this pursuit affect the broad network of interconnections that has evolved during Israeli rule?

Third: What impressions and judgments can be made on economic grounds about the "economic viability" arguments that will, by all evidence, continue to figure most prominently in political discourse and debate about the future of the West Bank and the Gaza Strip?

AN APPRAISAL OF MAJOR ECONOMIC EFFECTS

Two major characteristics define the economic relationship that has developed between Israel and the West Bank and the Gaza Strip—the growth of a market for local labor in Israel, and the growth of a market for Israeli commodities in the two territories. Quantitatively, these developments outweigh all other effects, which at least in the short term have been comparatively minor.

Economic links have been maintained between the West Bank and Jordan, and to a lesser extent between the Gaza Strip and Jordan. Because of the open bridges policy, trade has continued— particularly the West Bank's export of agricultural goods and products processed from agricultural inputs. However, this trade has substantially declined in relative significance. Important monetary and fiscal ties between the West Bank and Jordan have continued, creating the principal exception to the prevailing post-1967 pattern of progressively tighter connections between the territories and the Israeli economy.

Short-Term Effects

Some of the short-term effects are clear. The economic connections created between Israel and the two territories since 1967 have had a large expansionary effect in the West Bank and the Gaza Strip, generating a high rate of growth of income for the Palestinians, and drawing previously unemployed workers into active employment. For the Israeli economy also, the pattern of trade and access to cheap labor have been of considerable benefit.

Short-term costs have been discernible too. Some sectors of the West Bank and the Gaza Strip economies suffered from the immediate consequences of the Israeli occupation—for example, the West Bank tourist trade. It is more difficult to demonstrate persuasively that the withdrawal of labor from the West Bank and the Gaza Strip into Israel, in itself, has had immediate negative consequences on the local economies. But it is evident that, even in the short term, it must have created problems for some sectors.

The changed relationship between Jordan and the West Bank has also had its short-term costs and benefits. Most important has been the loss of tourist income, which before 1967 had been an important source of foreign exchange for Jordan. Because both the East and West Banks of pre-1967 Jordan were industrially underdeveloped, the immediate costs in terms of dislocation of internal markets resulting from the division of the country were less than would have been the case for a more complex economy, particularly as the flow of agricultural and agriculture-based products from the West Bank to Jordan was maintained after 1967. Also, from the East Bank viewpoint, the break was not as costly as some predicted, partly because pre-1967 investment had been concentrated on the East Bank. In practice, the Jordanian economy has performed very well since 1967. From the West Bank point of view, continuing access to the Jordanian market for its exports has been valuable, without imposing any economic burden on Jordan.

Long-Term Implications

The long-term implications of these developments, for all of the economies, involve more difficult questions. In particular, the division of labor that is developing within the region may relegate the residents of the West Bank and the Gaza Strip to the role of supplying unskilled or semi-skilled labor to the Israeli economy, either directly or through subcontracting. Moreover, the very fast rate of growth achieved by this pattern of development since 1967 will not be sustainable in the future as the pool of unemployed labor is fully utilized, and as the gap narrows between the wage levels of the West Bank and the Gaza Strip and the bottom of the Israeli wage scale. The danger then will be that the Palestinian workers will be concentrated at the lower end of the Israeli wage scale without the same income growth possibilities as they enjoyed in recent years.

The long-term consequences of such development for local economic activities within the West Bank and the Gaza Strip are less predictable. Because local industry does not enjoy the benefits of protection from Israeli competition, or access to Israeli subsidies, the growth of some sectors of the territories' economies will be stunted. The West Bank and the Gaza Strip had little in the way of industry in 1967, and there has been no observable shift in the economic structure towards industry since. The industrial sector's contribution to total output is minimal, and is likely to remain so if current economic policies are maintained.

There is, of course, a school of economic thought that judges such an absence of industry to be perfectly sensible. The argument is that any industry created with the support of heavy protection is of no benefit, and that the emerging regional division of labor is both rational and economically efficient. Such a view would be unacceptable to the leaders of most, if not all developing countries, who would identify the absence of industry as a defining characteristic of the colonial legacy. This difference of view cannot be resolved by an appeal to an undisputed scientific truth. Nevertheless, Palestinian opinion, critical of existing policies that perpetuate industrial backwardness in the West Bank and the Gaza Strip, reflects a viewpoint widely held in the Third World in general. And this opinion is based on a plausible interpretation of the nature of economic underdevelopment.

This is not to say that it would be feasible to create greatly expanded industry solely through protection for the local market, which is too small to provide a basis for self-sufficient industrialization. The creation of new industries in the West Bank and the Gaza Strip would require more than traditional policies of protection—it would require active policies to promote new markets outside the two territories. One direction to look for such markets would be in Jordan and farther afield in the Middle East. The same can be said for development in some parts of the service sector.

The long-term economic basis for trade with Jordan and the rest of the Middle East depends upon current and future investments in the territories. Before 1967 the trade between the West and East Banks in manufactured goods was very small because of the limited industrialization in both halves of Jordan. Industrial development in Jordan remains modest. Future industrial trade flowing from the West Bank and the Gaza Strip to Jordan and other parts of the Middle East would only come with accelerated programs of industrial investment and their coordination to ensure complementarity and thus the opportunity for trade.

In the industrial, agricultural, and service sectors, the West Bank and the Gaza Strip economies would incur serious potential costs from continued relative isolation from the rest of the Middle

East. It would restrict severely possibilities for planning, negotiation and individual business initiative that would establish for the two territories a suitable niche in the Middle East economy. However, the personal and financial connections between the West Bank and the Gaza Strip and other parts of the Middle East remain of considerable importance, although difficult to quantify precisely. The familial connections continue between West Bank and Gaza Strip Palestinians and Kuwait, Saudi Arabia, Egypt, as well as Jordan. Some workers have sought jobs in Jordan to replace those lost in Israel during the 1975 downturn in the Israeli economy. Employment elsewhere in the Middle East, and the resultant remittances flowing back in the West Bank and the Gaza Strip, remain important elements in the economic situation.

The long-term costs of limits on economic contact with the rest of the Middle East arising out of the current situation are hypothetical to the extent that they imply the creation of patterns of trade and economic cooperation beyond those that have existed until now. Yet if the pace of economic expansion throughout the Middle East continues at a lively rate, and if the region goes through a process of structural transformation, then the long-term costs of isolation for the two territories would take on growing significance.

For Israel the long-term implications of the emerging economic network are mixed. Over time, benefits would continue to flow from an expanded, protected market for Israeli products, but dependence on Palestinian labor would have increasingly serious social implications.

For Jordan the persistence of the existing situation is likely to mean that even if the trade and other connections mentioned above are retained, the relative economic importance of the West Bank connection will continue to decline. The trends evident since 1967 will be intensified, and trading relationships, which under other circumstances could have been expected to be increasingly important to the East Bank because of proximity and inherited economic ties, will remain relatively unimportant. Also, in the situation as it has existed since 1948, there is a continuing economic cost in Jordan's losing convenient access to the Mediterranean and having instead to rely on its southern port of Aqaba for sea access to the outside world.

To summarize: With more than one-third of the employed population of the West Bank and Gaza Strip working in Israel, and with as much as 50 percent of the territories' growth of income since 1967 attributable to wages earned in Israel, a connection has been created which is important on one side as a source of income and on the other as a source of labor. The access to markets in the West Bank and Gaza Strip has become significant in Israeli commercial life. Alongside these new links, economic connections with Jordan remain of importance, particularly to the West Bank. The export trade, while not growing, is still an important market for West Bank agriculture. The East Bank remains an actual and potential job market, and an important financial link.

ECONOMIC SELF-INTERESTS AND OPTIONS

This study has tried to show that although market forces stimulated the major changes affecting the West Bank and Gaza Strip economies, these forces have operated in a highly controlled environment. The resulting economic pattern has reflected key policy decisions, taken in the special political circumstances prevailing since 1967. It was observed at the outset of this chapter that changes in the political status of the two territories can no longer be contemplated seriously without also taking account of the economic constraints and opportunities associated with such political change. New political circumstances would inevitably open opportunities for different economic policies. How different these might be, and what alterations they might produce in the existing pattern of interconnections among the four economies, are questions whose answers would depend on the precise political scenario being assumed for the future. Furthermore, they would depend on the accompanying assumptions that are made about the availability of external finance, the domestic economic philosophies and foreign economic alignments of the various economies, the size and character of the population that the economy must mobilize and support, and other dimensions of economic policy.

Nevertheless, it is not necessary to identify and evaluate all desirable or feasible political scenarios in order to discuss the underlying economic interests that will be important from the viewpoint of the West Bank and the Gaza Strip economies. Nor is this necessary in order to discuss the major modifications in economic policy that would be required to respond to the specific economic needs of the West Bank and the Gaza Strip. It is only necessary, for the sake of this discussion, to posit that a number of basic economic interests are evident in the situation as it has developed since 1967 and to anticipate that efforts will be made to satisfy those interests if future political change facilitates economic strategies geared principally to promoting the well-being of the West Bank and Gaza Strip societies. Israeli economic policies toward the two territories during the past nine years have been most responsive, naturally enough, to Israeli interests—for example, limiting agricultural imports, restricting the inflow of commuting laborers from the territories when Israeli unemployment was high, and loosening these restrictions when economic expansion created demands for labor. How might a similar interplay of economic policies and self-interests evolve, as seen from the perspective of the West Bank and the Gaza Strip?

An examination of the interplay of economic interests from the perspective of the territories produces two overall conclusions. First: the most pervasive impact of the network of interconnections emerging since 1967 has been on the West Bank and the Gaza Strip, not on Israel or Jordan. Second: the purely economic interests of the two territories would be well-served by some major modifications in the prevailing network, and without such modifications and without reorientation of present trends, both territories' economies face a prospect of qualitative deterioration in some sectors.

Analysis in earlier chapters suggests that a policy responsive to the two territories' economic interests would most obviously gain by changing the existing trading relationship with Israel. Such a policy would have three elements: to protect or subsidize some branches of local industry against Israeli competition, to expose Israeli imports to competition with imports of other countries, and to develop markets for local products elsewhere in the Middle East.

"Normal" trading relationships in the international economy typically involve neither absolute free trade nor total isolation. Without being unmindful of the powerful influence of noneconomic factors that often determine whether the norm is achieved and whether the costs of either free trade or isolation are tolerable, it is possible to specify a range of trading policies that approximate the norm and that satisfy mutual economic interests of trading partners. In the case of the West Bank and the Gaza Strip, there would be little lost by a substantial reorientation away from the present trading connection with Israel, resulting in a lower level of penetration into local markets by Israeli goods. This lower level would be set as Israeli products are placed on the same footing as products from other potential sources, or as Israel is given privileged access to local markets in return for an appropriate *quid pro quo*. Although a rapid expansion of the present pattern of industrial subcontracting might establish a greater stake in the existing trade connections for some businessmen in the territories, reduced dependence on high-priced and highly protected Israeli sources of supply would benefit the local economies as a whole. However, there would be costs to the West Bank and the Gaza Strip if the Israeli trade were to disappear entirely. Obviously, the territories benefit from access to a transport system that handles some part of their external trade through Israel. And many Israeli products would be able to compete successfully with foreign imports even without protection, although price reductions might be needed to meet international competition.

The application of external tariffs to trade with Israel would not only reduce dependence on Israel as a source of supply, it also would provide an important fiscal resource for the territories, without necessarily eliminating the trade. On the other hand, trade with the rest of the Middle East could be expanded, although its dimensions are difficult to predict given the fast growth and high rate of structural change being experienced by Middle East economies. The geographical proximity of Israel and the West Bank and Gaza is such that in the absence of common trading area arrangements—but with normal trading access—*i.e.,* external tariffs for trade in both directions without a boycott—there would be the economic basis for an active trading relationship. But with the data available, it is not possible to judge what proportion of the existing trade would be continued.

Despite these uncertainties about the quantity of prospective trade between Israel and the territories, it is plausible that the territories' economic interests would make extensive involvement in foreign trade desirable. Natural resources are limited, and high levels of imports are therefore inevitable. Economic growth, moreover, would require imported capital equipment. The size of the local market is small enough that manufacturing development would have to be selective, and in many lines, exports would be necessary to achieve an acceptable level of efficiency.

The examination in previous chapters of the labor market connection between the territories and Israel suggests that the translation of the West Bank and the Gaza Strip economic interests into policy is less obvious in this sphere. The returns resulting from employment in Israel have been direct, immediate, and economic; whereas the costs are indirect, probably long-term, and in part social. On purely economic grounds, therefore, it is not clear what steps would be desirable to change this connection immediately. No doubt, however, if the connection were to continue, the economic interests of the commuting laborers would be well-served by new arrangements regarding status, terms and security of employment and similar matters.

More important though, the network of relationships in the labor sector will not be modified only by policies aimed directly at that objective. Policies aimed at changing the internal economies also will modify the external connection *indirectly*. Any programs that raise the rate of investment within the West Bank and the Gaza Strip and thereby expand local job opportunities would reduce dependence on the Israeli job market. Investment could well expand not only through the public sector but also through a willingness by West Bank and Gaza Strip residents to take advantage of new local investment opportunities, including the possibility of investments in protected or subsidized industrial and agricultural development. The prevailing high degree of dependence on job opportunities outside the territories, in other words, is a symptom of general local underdevelopment. Success in promoting more vigorous and balanced development within the two territories would remove the need for such dependence.

As is true for the trade connection, a total break of the labor connection between the two territories and Israel would impose costs on the local economies. It is probable that any total and immediate loss of employment opportunities in the Israeli economy would be a major depressant on the level of the economic activity in the West Bank and the Gaza Strip. However, in the medium term, the problem of alternative employment is less severe. Much of the labor is of a character which could be absorbed in public works programs and in jobs generated by fresh private investment if the finances and organizations were available. It is also possible that some of this labor can be absorbed in the Jordan labor market, as at least a temporary solution. But the conclusion is inescapable that expansion of productive jobs in the West Bank and the Gaza Strip would be required in the long term in order to absorb the workers displaced. This means accelerated development of industrial production—necessarily for both local and export markets—as well as in the service sectors, for there is little likelihood that the agricultural sector can re-absorb large numbers.

The redeployment of all those working in Israel at the peak employment level in 1974 would involve creating jobs for fewer than 100,000 workers. The recorded peak employment in 1974 was 79,000; even allowing for underestimation, the total would be less than 100,000. More recently, with the downturn in the Israeli economy, employment has slackened anyway. Nevertheless, redeployment would involve a massive effort in relation to the size of the local economy. Absorption of such numbers within the West Bank and Gaza Strip would require levels of investment at a totally different order of magnitude than the territories have experienced—although by standards of international comparison, an employment-generation target even of the illustrative figure of 100,000 is not enormous.

From an economic point of view, therefore, even if the policy objectives in the West Bank and the Gaza Strip were to eliminate dependence on the Israeli job market, and even if we were to suppose that public works and job-creating private investment would provide a partial medium-term solution, the long-term solution would require restructuring of the economies of the West Bank and the Gaza Strip.

Changes in economic structure to provide more job opportunities locally would require substantial investment. The judgment that expanded investment programs and local industrial development could provide a considerable expansion in local job opportunities can be offered here on qualitative grounds, if not with the necessary quantitative support. The relationship between the need for external finance and the initial creation of local jobs is that investment would require expanded imports. But as labor shifted into employment within the West Bank and the Gaza Strip, external earnings resulting from their work outside would decline. It is because some alternative source of finance for imports would be required until expanded local production either displaced imports or generated exports that the structural transformation of the West Bank and Gaza Strip economies would call for large external finance. At the same time, however, local savings have been considerable in recent years, so that in a political environment where economic policies were geared to promoting investment opportunities, locally-based capital accumulation would also be probable. The degree to which outside jobs could be replaced with local job opportunities, the likelihood and speed with which new export markets could be created, or imports replaced, to reduce the need for external finance—all would dictate the direction and pacing of economic planning and policy. This would be a time-consuming as well as expensive process. Thus the conclusion remains that whatever the long-term objectives and outcome, total disengagement from the Israeli labor market would have considerable short-term cost.

Finally, analysis in earlier chapters suggests that West Bank and Gaza Strip economic interests in the monetary and fiscal spheres raise rather different issues for the local economies in view of the limited ties to Israel that have evolved in these sectors. At a minimum, what can be said is that the immediate interests of the territories would be to restore a normal commercial banking system that serves both public and private requirements in the territories, and that serves as an essential adjunct to expanding economic and commercial transactions. This objective, in itself, would involve relatively little adjustment of interests with Israel, given the lack of present integration in this sector—in contrast to the trade and labor sectors. Rather—in view of the large and varied connections retained particularly by the West Bank with Jordan in this sphere—it involves a management of fiscal and monetary interests affecting Amman and the local economies. These interests will come into play inevitably during the course of any future decisions setting, for the two territories, currency policy, public spending and taxation programs—indeed the full range of other monetary and fiscal measures that are so inherently bound up with the exercise of political authority.

An examination of the interplay of economic interests in these sectors, as they appear from the perspective of the Israeli economy, also produces two overall conclusions. First: The network of interconnections emerging since 1967 has had a major effect on the structure and performance of the West Bank and Gaza Strip economies, but less significant effect on the Israeli economy in relative terms and more selective in impact. Second: Apart from savings on the cost side of the Israeli budget balance for the two territories, any major modification of the existing pattern of interconnections with the territories is nevertheless likely to result in disadvantage to some elements in the Israeli economy.

In general, especially between 1967 and 1973, Israel reaped economic advantages by tapping a new market and a new source of labor in the West Bank and the Gaza Strip. But this process has had selective rather than comprehensive importance for the economy of Israel, and the principal thrust of Israel's economic growth during those years has not depended on the connection with the territories. In the aggregate, the significance of this economic connection to the territories is still only a minor part of the total Israeli economic picture. Israel's strictly economic interests in this connection lead to a probable preference that any reorientation of relationships should be both gradual and partial.

Restrictions on Israeli exports to the two territories, or the loss of Israel's privileged status vis-à-vis other potential export sources, or encouragement in the territories of production that would compete with that of Israeli suppliers—all such measures would mean costs to Israeli exporters for whom the territories have become a leading market in recent years, albeit a market sustained, in turn, by incomes earned in Israel. Given the time required to develop alternative markets, the Israeli economic interest would be to avoid any abrupt modification of the established trading relationship. Likewise, major modifications in Israeli access to labor would impose burdens on the Israeli economy, both in the loss of labor-policy flexibility and in the adjustments that would have to be made in those sectors, especially construction, now most dependent on commuting labor from the territories. Of course, the level of the burden would depend both on the magnitude of any modification and on the cyclical state of the Israeli economy—for the latter reason, labor would have been missed less in 1975-76 than in 1974. And if the labor connection were to be maintained but with new arrangements protecting the terms of employment and status of the commuting workers, these arrangements would probably have to be made at some cost to competitive groups of Israeli laborers—but the overall costs to Israel would not be great.

In sum, extreme and abrupt modifications of existing labor and trade relationships with the territories would not serve Israel's economic interests. Such modifications, while not spelling a major economic crisis for Israel, would impose high costs and would require selective reorientation of the economy. On the other hand, there have not been major investments by Israel in West Bank or Gaza Strip industrial capacity or infrastructure, and to a degree the absence of such investments makes the existing overall pattern of economic connections more easily alterable or reversible. There has not been extensive investment in specific economic projects whose enduring productivity is contingent on maintenance of the connection between Israel and the territories. And there has not been any substantial pattern of inter-industry ties created between the territories and Israel, involving integration of industrial processes between the economies. For all of these reasons, there are few direct economic stakes in the territories that, in themselves, would leave Israel dependent upon economic developments in the West Bank and the Gaza Strip.

What the preceding exploration warrants is a provisional judgment. The interplay of economic interests since 1967 among the economies of Israel, the West Bank, and the Gaza Strip has not yet carried economic integration to a point where it becomes impossible to unscramble the economies and modify their relationships in mutually beneficial ways without imposing intolerable burdens on any one economy. There is a spectrum of economically plausible possibilities available to transform the links characterizing the existing economic situation, should political developments call for a transformation. Some possibilities are better, economically, than others for one or the other economy, or for groups within them. Some mixes of possibilities come closer than others to our hypothetical pattern of "normal" economic relationships, amounting neither to isolation nor to uncontrolled integration, but to a network of mutually beneficial transactions, limited and controlled by each economic partner to defend particular economic self-interests. To repeat: How far from this norm a balance can be struck will depend predominantly on political calculations and intentions.

ECONOMIC VIABILITY

The terms of reference for this study do not include an economic assessment of specific alternative political scenarios for the future of the West Bank and the Gaza Strip, and these terms of reference will not be exceeded here. But for reasons set out in the opening of this final chapter, economic arguments, particularly arguments about "economic viability," are increasingly finding their way into political discourse about what is desirable or possible regarding the future of these two territories. The overall analysis in this and preceding chapters does not provide—or profess to provide—an answer to the frequently-voiced question of whether an independent state made up of the West Bank and the Gaza Strip could in some sense be "economically viable." What the analysis does provide, however, is a way of looking at the question and what it means.

It must be emphasized at the outset that economists have no satisfactory definition of the phrase "economic viability," whether the term is applied to the Middle East or elsewhere. Indeed, a glance at the work of careful economists who have tried to apply it to the West Bank and the Gaza Strip makes clear how slippery a notion it is. One study of the economic viability of a West Bank state affirms the ambiguity of the concept:

> If economic viability refers to a basic independence of foreign aid, then few developing nations would be considered to be economically viable. If the term implies a reduction in the balance-of-payments deficit, again few countries would be viable. Viability might be measured by the development effort of a country: this would involve measuring the ratio of investment to GNP or the ratio of investment to total available resources. It would seem that most frequently writers imply that economic viability involves rapid growth of production and income accompanied by a reduction in unemployment—that is, a period in which a country strives to reach a point at which balance-of-payments and budgetary deficits begin to decline thereby reducing dependence on foreign aid. [1]

This same study, however, goes on to adopt a working definition of the concept that itself shows how difficult it is to resolve the ambiguity satisfactorily:

> A country will be regarded as economically viable if its economic characteristics permit it to experience sustained economic growth and rising welfare per capita and if its economic processes function well enough to permit a modicum of social and political stability; conversely, economic viability requires political and economic conditions that permit growth and development. [2]

In an earlier study prepared just after the 1967 Middle East war, another economist discusses the effects of the loss of the West Bank on the Jordan economy, and raises the issue of whether Jordan after 1967 could be considered "viable." [3] Noting that the term is "widely used, though ill-defined," he points out, correctly, that if the tests of viability are independence from aid, gradual reduction in the balance of payments deficits, or capital formation effort, then Jordan was not "viable" *even before* 1967, although it had achieved high rates of growth in product and income. [4] Similarly, as the economic history of Israel would show if these tests were applied to it, there is a sense in which that country has not been "viable" by some measures. Indeed, both Israel and Jordan over the past generation have been among the world's leading recipients of external assistance, both in absolute terms and, more importantly, in proportion to the total level of domestic economic activity.

To ask, "Could a West Bank-Gaza Strip state be viable?" is to pose the wrong question. For this, as for other territory about which the question might be asked, the answer is neither "Yes" nor "No." The only realistic answer is "Only if. . . . " Very few economies could be successful in theory under conditions of autarky. Virtually none are in practice. Neither theory nor experience tells us very much about the economic consequences of the size of nations *per se*. Economic potential is not a function only of fixed geographic characteristics, or resource bases, or other inherent natural features such as climate and so on—even though these features may well have to do with the nature of economic life that the occupants of a piece of real estate manage to sustain. Many economies exist which, on *a priori* reasoning might seem economically implausible, that is, unable to provide their population with a satisfactory livelihood. Some of these survive without much success; others do well under extraordinarily adverse conditions.

It is evident from this study that since 1967 the West Bank and the Gaza Strip have had their economic prospects shaped in large measure—though not exclusively—by the nature of the labor, trade, and monetary-fiscal external connections linking the territories to other economies. *In principle* this will continue to be true for the territories under alternative political futures. It may or it may not be the same interconnections that now exist; but *some* external economic interconnections, most probably major ones, will be an essential foundation for economic life in the territories. Which interconnections, with whom, how intensive—all are questions that will help mold the quality of economic life in the territories, as will the population-base, development strategies, and other basic elements in the economic picture.

At the very least, it seems unpersuasive to assert on economic grounds alone that economic life in the West Bank and Gaza Strip could no longer continue if the territories possessed wider leeway to define and pursue their own economic self-interests, and that nothing economically satisfactory could replace the existing situation. Indeed the existing situation itself may be economically disadvantageous for the territories over the long term for the reasons suggested in this study. But it also must be added that, despite this long-term structural prognosis, the people of the West Bank and the Gaza Strip are currently participating in an active and ongoing daily economic life in a reasonably adequate immediate economic environment. And they are enjoying per capita incomes which are respectable by accepted international standards—this without extraordinary flows of external assistance

This study's review of the economic consequences of Israel's rule over the West Bank and the Gaza Strip points to no single, simple verdict. For the Palestinian residents of the two territories, the past nine years have brought a modicum of economic well-being—but the agenda of steps needed to move toward balanced and sustained economic development remains formidable, and the legacy of these years has done little to remedy basic structural problems that continue to characterize the economies of both territories. For the Israeli, West Bank, Gaza Strip, and Jordanian economies considered together, these years have produced a new network of economic interdependencies—but the continuation of this network in the event of any prospective political change in the status of the territories promises to be highly controversial on both economic and political grounds. And, finally, for those who have been concerned about how and whether Israeli coexistence with the Palestinians of the two territories could be advanced by economic policies, these years have shown that economic normalization can be achieved under the most difficult conditions—but any such normalization in itself cannot ameliorate the underlying political problems in the conflict between Israel and the Palestinians.

Footnotes

1. Vivian Bull, *The West Bank—Is it Viable?* (Lexington, Massachusetts: D. C. Heath and Company, 1975), p. 12.

2. *Ibid.,* pp. 12-13.

3. Eliyahu Kanovsky, *The Economic Impact of the Six-Day War* (New York: Praeger, 1970), pp. 424-425.

4. *Ibid.,* p. 422.

APPENDIX I

The Measurement of Real Growth

The major difficulty of measuring the growth trend achieved in the West Bank and the Gaza Strip is the uncertainty about an appropriate baseline for measurement. In 1968 when the Israeli statistical series on the product of the territories begins, the economic life of the West Bank and the Gaza Strip had not yet recovered from the immediate economic effects of disruption resulting from the 1967 war. Some of the subsequent growth was therefore simply recovery, rather than net expansion in the productive performance of the economies.

However, it is difficult to find an alternative baseline. There are several problems in measuring growth as compared to the prewar situation:

(a) National product statistical series were not available for the territories prior to 1967; economic activity on the West Bank was incorporated in the Jordanian national accounts.

(b) Although there are estimates of the situation in 1965-66, they do not have the same geographical coverage because they include East Jerusalem.

(c) There was also a major population shift, with the flight of Arabs from the West Bank and Gaza Strip. It is impossible to assess the implications of this migration for the capacity to produce.

Table A-I

Pre-1967 Resource Availability
(In Millions of Jordanian Dinars)

West Bank (1965)	
Gross national product (factor cost)	54.5
Net import surplus	11.5
The Gaza Strip (1966)	
Gross national product	9.6
Net import surplus	2.9

SOURCE: Haim Ben Shahar, Eitan Berglas, Yair
Mundlak and Ezra Sadan, *Economic
Structure and Development Prospects of the
West Bank and the Gaza Strip* (Santa
Monica, California: Rand, 1971), pp. 26, 29
and 31.

(d) The change in political regime was combined with a partial change in the currency and changes in relative prices.

With the available data, there is no way that estimates of growth can be fully reliable and precise. The calculations made here do not profess to be "better" or "more reliable" than those already available; these calculations merely suggest a range over which estimates can quite legitimately vary under plausible assumptions.

Our starting point must be the estimates made in 1967 by the Israeli authorities of the income and product of the West Bank and the Gaza Strip in 1965 and 1966. The results are set out in Table A-I. Other estimates suggested that West Bank participation in Jordanian GNP was greater than the one-third these figures suggest. Mazur estimates as much as 40 percent.[1] Ward writes that in 1966, 38 percent of Jordanian GNP originated in the West Bank,[2] basing his estimates upon the Jordanian GNP figures in a "U.S. Embassy Report." Kanovsky, however, plausibly argues that the Israeli estimates are not too cautious—indeed he suggests that "it must be considered a maximum."[3]

However, even if all or any of these figures are acceptable, several difficulties remain. Published figures included the estimated output of East Jerusalem, which was later excluded from the West Bank data following the Israeli government's annexation, and are at price levels which are difficult to relate to the post-1967 price levels.[4]

In September, 1967, the population of East Jerusalem was recorded at 65,857, some 10 percent of the total population then remaining on the West Bank. Taking the 1965 East Jerusalem population as about 10 percent of West Bank population, what proportion of the West Bank GNP would we expect to have come from East Jerusalem?

The Israelis estimated that the GNP of the West Bank (including East Jerusalem) was 545 million Israeli pounds in 1965,[5] compared to an estimated GNP for the West Bank (excluding East Jerusalem), in 1968 (at prices of that year) of 330 million Israeli pounds. Allowing for a modest price rise of 12 percent—the 1965-68 rise in the Israeli consumer price index (CPI)—the comparison (at 1965 prices) is between 295 million Israeli pounds (1968 West Bank GNP at 1965 prices) and 545 million Israeli pounds (1965 West Bank GNP including East Jerusalem). The difference—that is, 45 percent of the combined GNP—could not be explained on the basis of any likely East Jerusalem product; 1968 output must therefore have been considerably below prewar peaks.

Alternatively, one can work back from the assertion of Shahar and his colleagues[6] that per capita produce was 7 percent higher in 1968 than before the war, although the basis for this conclusion is unexplained. This method suggests a level of GNP for the West Bank (excluding East Jerusalem) of about 420 million Israeli pounds (at 1968 prices) prior to the war. The reason why a *lower* per capita GNP gives rise to a *higher* total GNP is that the population was much higher before 1967. For this to be true, the income of East Jerusalem would need to be 31 percent of the total West Bank and East Jerusalem product. (For details, see Table A-II.)

While it is not possible to resolve this problem on the basis of information available, data from Israeli sources indicates that the level of West Bank GNP in 1968 was significantly below the prewar level. That the growth in gross national product (at constant prices) was 21 percent in 1968-69 for the West Bank itself suggests that 1968 levels did not represent recovery from the 1967 disruption. Recovery of product levels per capita would not indicate very much as the migration of 200,000-300,000[7] of the poorest inhabitants as a result of the 1967 war should by itself have raised the per capita income of the West Bank.

Table A-II

Calculation of Alternative Estimate of Real Growth, the West Bank and the Gaza Strip

Step I   Adjustment of West Bank Output

i   Estimate of output in 1965 (gross
     national product at factor cost)*   = 545 million Israeli pounds
                                                 (conversion rate of 1
                                                 dinar = 10 Israeli pounds

ii   Reduction of 20 percent to allow for
     separation of East Jerusalem leaves** = 436 million Israeli pounds

iii Allowing for a 13 percent price rise
     1965-68***   = 493 million Israeli pounds in
                                             1968 prices

This compares to the estimated GNP at factor cost for the West Bank in 1968 of 330 million Israeli pounds. That is, the GNP of the West Bank was some *one-third* below 1965 levels in 1968.

Step II   Estimated 1968 Output Capacity

Adjusted West Bank GNP (factor cost)   493 million Israeli pounds
Actual Gaza Strip GNP (factor cost)   128

Adjusted base for estimating growth   621 million Israeli pounds

---

*   This is based on the estimate of 54.5 million dinars for 1965 of the West
      Bank's gross national product published in Economic Planning Authority,
      Economic Survey of the West Bank (Jerusalem: 1967), p. 9. In the
      English summary of this survey, a figure of 60.3 million dinars is given as
      an estimate for 1966 gross national product, so that an even higher
      figure might be justified for this calculation. See Economic Planning
      Authority, *Economic Survey of the West Bank* (Summary) (Jerusalem:
      Prime Minister's Office, 1967), Table 3, p. 7.

Footnotes

1. Michael P. Mazur, "Economic Development of Jordan" in Charles A. Cooper and Sidney Alexander, eds., *Economic Development and Population Growth in the Middle East* (New York: American Elsevier, 1972), p. 240.

2. Richard Ward, "The Economics of a Palestine Entity" in Don Peretz, Evan M. Wilson and Richard J. Ward, *A Palestine Entity?* (Washington, D.C.: The Middle East Institute, 1970), p. 180.

3. Eliyahu Kanovsky, *The Economic Impact of the Six-Day War* (New York: Praeger, 1970), pp. 394-395.

Step III   Output Level 1973

Gross National Product (Factor Cost)
(In Millions of Israeli Pounds)

	1973 Current Prices	1968 Prices
West Bank	1307	643
Gaza	736	308
Total	2043	951

Step IV   Adjusted Growth Rate

$$\frac{951}{621} = 153.1 = 9 \text{ percent per annum}$$

** As explained above, there is no evidence regarding the precise contribution of East Jerusalem. This estimate weights its economic contribution higher than its relative weight in the 1967 West Bank population.

*** Implicit GNP price deflator, 1965-68, for the Israeli economy. It may be assumed that this is a very conservative estimate of price increases actually experienced in the West Bank. These GNP deflators are derived from the data in Table xxvi/7, p. 689 of the *Statistical Abstract of Israel 1975*, which is a later source than for the other GNP figures shown in this study. It is used because it contains a constant price series at 1968 prices for GNP which became available too late to adjust all the other tables in the study. GNP at factor cost in 1968 prices is derived by using the implicit deflators for GNP at market price.

4. Kanovsky, *op. cit.*, p. 167, cites evidence that East Jerusalem prices rose a maximum of 50 percent from May, 1967, to May, 1969.

5. This figure is from Haim Ben Shahar, E. Berglas, Y. Mundlak and E. Sadan, *Economic Structure and Development Prospects of the West Bank and the Gaza Strip* (Santa Monica, California: The Rand Corporation, 1971, pp. 25-27. The authors use an exchange rate of ten Israeli pounds to one Jordanian dinar.

7. The amount of population movement also has been subject to varying estimates. Mazur says "some 300,000" (*op. cit.*, p. 239); Kanovsky says "about 200,000-250,000" (*op. cit.*, p. 145); while Arie Bregman (*Economic Growth in the Administered Areas, 1968-1973* [Jerusalem: Bank of Israel Research Department, 1975], p. 27), Vivian Bull (*The West Bank—Is It Viable?* [Lexington, Massachusetts: D. C. Heath and Co., 1975], p. 112), and Ward (*op. cit.*, p. 108) all quote a figure of 250,000.

APPENDIX II

Estimates of the Impact of Foreign Earnings

In estimating the multiplier effect of the growth in foreign earnings on aggregate expenditure in the West Bank and Gaza Strip, account is taken of the propensity to consume, the propensity to import and the degree to which foreign earnings substitute for domestic income.

Where:

c = marginal propensity to consume

m = marginal propensity to import out of consumption spending

t = proportion of foreign earnings which substitute for domestic earnings

the multipler formula is: $\dfrac{1-t}{1-c+cm}$

Using the figures in Table A-III, a multiplier of 1.5 was arrived at, assuming zero substitution of foreign for domestic income. If such substitution were, say, 20 percent of the foreign earnings, the multiplier would be reduced accordingly to 1.2.

These figures are not reliable enough to give us more than a rough idea of orders of magnitude.

Rough Calculation of Consumption and Import Propensities

	West Bank and Gaza Strip Combined (In Millions of Israeli Pounds at Current Prices)		Increase
	1968	1973	1968-1973
1. Gross disposable private income from all sources*	567	2157	1590
2. Private consumption expenditure	501	1691	1190
3. Imports of goods and services (including taxes on imports)	303	1195	892

	Average Propensities		Incremental Propensity
Rough estimate of consumption propensity (2/1)	.88	.78	.75
Rough estimate of import propensity (3/1)**	.53	.55	.56

Taking c = 0.75 and m = 0.56

$$\frac{1}{1-c+cm} = 1.5$$

---

* Defined as gross national product (at factor cost) plus transfers from government and local authorities minus income tax and transfer to the government plus private transfers from abroad.

** This is a very rough estimate. It relates total imports to gross disposable private income, as there is no way of identifying the proportion of imports of goods and services utilized by government or for investment purposes.

SOURCE: *Quarterly Statistics of the Administered Territories, Vol. IV, Nos. 3-4* (Jerusalem: Central Bureau of Statistics, 1974), pp. 77, 79, 85.